BEARS
ESSENTIAL

Everything You Need to Know to Be a Real Fan!

David Claerbaut

TRIUMPH
BOOKS
CHICAGO

Library of Congress Cataloging-in-Publication Data

Claerbaut, David.
    Bears essential : everything you need to know to be a real fan! / David Claerbaut.
        p. cm.
    ISBN-13: 978-1-57243-843-9
    ISBN-10: 1-57243-843-6
    1. Chicago Bears (Football team)—History. I. Title.

GV956.C5C58 2006
796.323'640977311—dc22

                                                                2006007648

This book is available in quantity at special discounts for your group or organization. For further information, contact:

Triumph Books
542 South Dearborn Street
Suite 750
Chicago, Illinois 60605
(312) 939-3330
Fax (312) 663-3557

Printed in U.S.A.
ISBN-13: 978-1-57243-843-9
ISBN-10: 1-57243-843-6
Design by Patricia Frey
All photos courtesy of AP/Wide World Photos except where otherwise indicated.

To Roger and my son Chris,
a pair of true believers
in more ways than one.

Contents

Foreword

Somewhere in the back of my mind, I can hear that song playing on a continuous loop. That song is "Bear Down, Chicago Bears," as it can only be sung at Soldier Field, with the faithful fans of the beloved Bears in full voice on a frigid wintry day. That's when you know what it is like to be a Bears fan.

The first time I rolled into Chicago more than three decades ago and caught a glimpse of Lake Shore Drive, I became awestruck approaching the magnificent pillars and arches adorning Soldier Field. Oh, the memories of the great players who performed on that field! Not to mention the many Hall of Fame NFL stars who played at Wrigley Field before the Bears shifted their home games to Soldier Field.

NFL pioneer and Bears founder George Halas created a lasting American institution, and I am proud to have had some small part in it as a player, as a fan, and as a broadcaster. From the first time I met Coach Halas to the last time we sat down and talked just before his passing, I realized he had the heart of a wonderful, caring man. I will never forget him calling out to me—and to every other player who dared walk into the old executive offices at 55 East Jackson: "I want to see you before you go!"

That meant he wanted to check up on you and find out where your life was headed. It meant that he truly cared about each one of us as individuals.

Coach Halas had a unique way of surrounding himself with special, dedicated people. Sid Luckman, Dick Butkus, Mike Ditka, Gale Sayers, Walter Payton... Oh, the stories there are to be told. Stories that have become part of the fabric of the lives of Chicago sports fans and observers.

As superb as the players have been throughout Bears history, it has been the fans who have made the game of professional football what it is today. The sounds, the smells, the frigid temperatures...Bears fans know what I am talking about when it comes to the team's incredible lore. Now you have a wonderful opportunity to sit back, relax, and enjoy this book that reminds us all how fortunate we are to be Chicago Bears fans.

—Dan Jiggetts

A Great Franchise

The Chicago Bears. The very name exudes power. It rings with dominance, force, might—intimidation. Not just the Bears, but the Chicago Bears—the football team from Carl Sandburg's city of the "Big Shoulders," from Al Capone's town, from the snowy and tough cold of the midwestern city by the lake. The Bears are the growling, fierce, vicious grown-up counterparts of Chicago's baseball Cubs. The Cubs are about lovable losers and fun in the sunshine; the Bears are about simple life-is-tough values, hard work, and grind-it-out success.

And they have been here forever. At least as long as modern recorded pro football history. The franchise was founded in 1919 in Decatur, Illinois, where the team played for only one year, 1920. By 1921 this charter member of what was to become the National Football League was in Chicago, where it has remained. Let the Oilers become the Titans, the Browns the Ravens, and let the Cardinals, Rams, Raiders, and Colts be the football versions of movable feasts. The Bears are the Bears, and they belong to Chicago where they have been as stable and rock solid a franchise as any in the NFL. The Chicago Bears, through 2005, have had only 13 coaches in 86 years.

And never mind the domed circus tents that are passed off as stadiums, the artificial surfaces that come and go, and the exploding scoreboards and other hi-tech electronic shows that now typify life in the NFL, distracting the fans from the game on the field. Since moving to Chicago in 1921, the team has played in essentially two stadiums, Wrigley Field and Soldier Field. Both are outdoor, no-frills venues, vulnerable to chilly lake winds off nearby Lake Michigan and snowy surfaces typical of Chicago winters. Bears fans come to watch the Bears.

TRIVIA

George Halas was an outstanding player. What position did he play?

Answers to the trivia questions are on pages 182–183.

Their colors are simple and cold—a bright orange set against a navy blue. And they are never altered. The helmet logo has been almost unchanging as well—an orange wishbone *C* with a navy blue backdrop. The team logo features a growling bear with facial highlights. The Chicago Bears. The Monsters of the Midway. The powerful, physical, stubborn, meat-and-potatoes football team that calls chilly temperatures "Bear weather." And the team has lived up to its image. Over the years the Bears have built their reputation on grudging, even violent, defense—led by rugged linemen, ferocious linebackers, and teeth-rattling secondary men—and a crunching ground game featuring crushing blockers and hard interior runners rather than slick quarterbacks and acrobatic wide receivers. Even their most notable coaches reflect the franchise's image. The Cleveland Browns had the erudite Paul Brown, the Bears had George Halas, the 49ers had the sophisticated Bill Walsh, and the Bears had Iron Mike Ditka.

The gridiron brainchild of Papa Bear George Stanley Halas, the Bears came out of their lair with ferocity right from the start, winning the first pro football championship in 1921. Throughout the '20s they were a dominant force on the pro football landscape. Franchises came and went, rose and fell, but the Bears pushed on, posting winning seasons in 24 of their first 25 years of existence. By 1950 the Chicago Bears had won seven NFL titles. On three other occasions they came up short only in the championship game. In short, the Bears symbolized the NFL at its best and toughest. They were the yardstick against which other teams and franchises measured themselves.

Despite some bleak years in succeeding decades, the franchise had an all-time record of 660–489–42 going into the 2005 season, 171 games over .500.

Nearly half of those wins were registered by the personification of the Bears, George Halas, the bespectacled owner, forever wearing a hat on a head that sported a flat nose and a face that looked like a clenched fist. It was the indomitable, seemingly indestructible Halas who for more than five decades towered over the wrecks of football time.

The Bears moved into Soldier Field, shown here in 1963 for a college field game, in 1971. The stadium was renovated in 2002 and reopened for play in 2003.

TRIVIA

Why are the Bears' colors orange and blue?

Answers to the trivia questions are on pages 182–183.

Halas and his successors had tremendous players, legendary gridiron greats. The Bears have had more than 30 Hall of Fame football players. There were tough guys with tough names like Bronko Nagurski, Doug Atkins, Bill George, Mike Ditka, Dick Butkus, and Mike Singletary, and other talented superstars like Sid Luckman, Red Grange, Gale Sayers, and Walter Payton. With these and all the other men who have worn the orange and blue, it has been more guts than glitz, more grunts than glory.

The new millennium will bring new Bears legends, on the field and on the coaching sideline. So much of life is about showing up, enduring, and then triumphing. That is the story of pro football—mean, tough, enduring, and ultimately overcoming. That is the Chicago Bears.

Birth of the Bears

The roots of pro football date back to the late 1800s, at least since William "Pudge" Heffelfinger received payment for his services on the Allegheny Athletic Association team in Pittsburgh. Heffelfinger was paid $500 in 1892. In those years various "athletic clubs" sprang up in Pennsylvania and Ohio, two states that have continued to be breeding grounds for gridiron stars. Town teams played town teams in what were essentially local, small-town rivalries, and players floated from team to team and even across state lines. Two Ohio towns were prominent in the development of the game, Canton—the current home of the Pro Football Hall of Fame—and Massillon, a city renowned for the finest in high school football.

After several decades of at best loosely organized professional and semiprofessional activity, a situation in which teams emerged and vanished, players went to the highest bidders, and an absence of control over how the game was being played existed, there was a widespread desire to form a league in which all members would follow the same rules.

A focused effort at organization failed in 1904, but 16 years later a meeting of interested teams was held in August. On September 17, 1920, a second meeting was convened in Canton, Ohio. The location was not an accident. Canton was the home of the famous Canton Bulldogs, for whom the great Jim Thorpe played, with Massillon, home of the Massillon, Ohio, Tigers only seven miles west of Canton. It was a most significant event, with representatives of teams from five different states in attendance. What made it even more significant is that in 1920, and for decades previous, America had but one national pastime, baseball. The summer game, with the likes of Babe Ruth, Ty Cobb, and Rogers Hornsby looming large, was already big league, and with no counterpart in the fall or winter.

Three Bears greats from the 1920s are shown here being inducted into the Pro Football Hall of Fame in 1964: Ed Healey (seated, second from left), James G. Conzelman (standing, second from left), and George Trafton (standing, far right).

Among the teams represented in Canton was the Decatur (Illinois) Staleys Athletic Club, or the Staleys.

The league was named the American Professional Football Association, with Jim Thorpe named league president. An entry fee was set at $100 to give the appearance of true professional respectability, although no team ever anted up. Each team did, however, agree to print "Member of American Professional Association" on its stationery. The team played for a silver cup, presented by a Mr. Marshall of the Brunswick-Balke Collender Company, Tire Division. Three straight championships gave a team ownership of the otherwise traveling cup.

The Staley Starch Company of Decatur, Illinois, was owned by a man named A. E. Staley. Staley asked one of his plant workers, a 25-year-old man named George Stanley Halas, to organize a football team. Promising a sufficient budget to attract quality players, Staley permitted the team to practice on company time.

Halas worked hard at assembling a competitive squad, picking up some real ringers. He signed end Guy Chamberlin, halfback Jimmy Conzelman, and center George Trafton, each of whom was later selected to the Pro Football Hall of Fame along with Halas, who was a topflight bothways end. He also acquired halfback Ed "Dutch" Sternaman and quarterback Charlie Dressen. When the enterprising Halas contacted Canton owner-manager Ralph Hay about scheduling a game against his illustrious Bulldogs, Hay did Halas one better. He informed him of a plan to organize a professional football league. As a result, Halas and the Staleys were cut in on the formation of the new league, and the Chicago Bears—although that name and location would come later—were born.

The 1920 edition of the American Professional Football Association, though now a formal league, needed a good deal of tightening. Teams played as many nonleague members as members, in contests conducted in minor league baseball parks or open venues with circus bleachers, facilities that separated standing fans from the on-field action by a rope. The game was popular at the local level, stirring considerable fervor in a pre-television era. Watching the town football team in the fall was a wonderfully pleasant and exciting outing for the fans, who, due to their ruralistic mind-set, were fiercely loyal to the local municipality.

Owing to near random scheduling, the inaugural season of the new league had everything but a satisfactory way of crowning a champion. Confusion reigned as Akron, Buffalo, and Canton all laid claim to the prized laurels. A series of games was planned to resolve the issue, but due to all-too-hasty arrangement and lack of effective follow-through, the games never eventuated. Clearly fans were thirsty for pro football, because more than 15,000 rooters showed up at New York's Polo Grounds to watch the Bulldogs take on the Buffalo All-Americans. The game went to Buffalo, 7–3, largely because the Buffalo squad stuffed a Thorpe punt and fell on the ball in the end zone. Thorpe hit on one of three field-goal attempts, but was described by writers in attendance as having slowed considerably from his halcyon days.

One other team adjudged itself the American Professional Association champion—the Decatur Staleys. The Illinois squad went 10–1–2 and based its case on having battled the undefeated Akron Pros to a scoreless tie in the teams' only confrontation.

TOP TEN

Greatest Bears Seasons

1. 1985 (15–1–0)—One game short of a perfect Super Bowl championship season.
2. 1941 (10–1–0)—Outscored opposition by better than 2-1 margin (396–147) in championship season.
3. 1942 (11–0–0)—Although coming up short in title game (14–6 at Washington), were undefeated in regular season, giving up just 84 points and tallying 376.
4. 1963 (11–1–2)—Championship season in which team dethroned Lombardi's Packers and prevailed against great Giants team in title tilt.
5. 1943 (8–1–1)—Scoring 303 points and yielding but 157, team crushed Washington 41–21 for NFL championship.
6. 1934 (13–0–0)—Lost championship game to Giants on frozen field after outscoring opposition 286–86 in unbeaten regular season.
7. 1940 (8–3–0)—Obliterated Washington 73–0 to win fourth NFL championship.
8. 1933 (10–2–1)—Snuck past the Giants 23–21 to win third NFL crown.
9. 1946 (8–2–1)—Hardly a dominating team, Bears took NFL title in a 24–14 Luckman-led win in New York.
10. 1948 (10–2–0)—Pounded foe's 375–151 point margin despite losing Western title 24–21 to Cardinals in final game of the season.

Halas was resourceful, employing a variety of innovative formations to befuddle the opposition. The T formation was his favorite, one in which he had played during his college days under Bob Zuppke at Illinois. Obviously, the game was a far cry from the one we know today. There was no training camp and weeks of preseason conditioning and drills. Instead, players showed up a week before the season began, practicing every day in the afternoons during the regular season. There were only about 16 players on a team, and substitutions were rare, usually made only if a player got hurt. Getting hurt meant something different as well. Players generally did not leave the field unless carried off on a stretcher. Playing through a broken nose or sprained ankle was not uncommon. The equipment was bare bones as well, as face masks and bulky shoulder pads

TRIVIA

On which street is the Hall of Fame located?

Answers to the trivia questions are on pages 182–183.

were quite a few years away. Pay was around $150 a game for the stars, much less for everyone else. But the games had a wild, ungoverned nature to them that the players and fans enjoyed. Bears quarterback Joey Sternaman remembers a bizarre play from the time that underscores this. "Our fullback, Oscar Knop, intercepted a pass and took off for the goal line, only it was the wrong goal line he was racing toward. It was in a game against the Columbus Tigers. The ball bounced off the chest of the intended receiver and into the arms of Knop, who somehow got turned around on the play. The entire Tiger team just stood there and watched as he started running the wrong way. Most of them were laughing." Eventually his teammate, Ed Healey, ran him down and tackled him at the 2-yard line, saving Knop from the distinction of being the first player to score points for the other team.

As for the fiscal side of the franchise, the struggling Staleys managed to pay each player the then-whopping sum of $1,900 for the season.

As 1920 closed, certainly the aggressive, young football fanatic George Stanley Halas never imagined that this auspicious start, on the field and at the cashbox, would only be the prelude to a more than six-decade association with one of the greatest sports franchises in the nation's history, one with which he would be inextricably linked, one that would neither be from Decatur, nor be called Staleys.

Papa Bear

Every Chicago Bears fan knows who Papa Bear is. George Stanley Halas is Papa Bear for two reasons. First, because—at 25 years of age—he was the founding father of the Chicago Bear family. Though representing the interests of A. E. Staley, it was Halas who attended the league's organizational meeting in Canton, Ohio, in 1920. That's good enough. Secondly, however, he was the heart and soul of the Chicago Bears from the 1920s to the 1980s. In fact, Halas could well be called Papa NFL, because no figure in the now glorious history of the NFL loomed as large for as long as did George Stanley Halas.

Halas was born in Chicago on February 2, 1895. He attended Crane Tech High School in the Windy City and the University of Illinois, where he played under Bob Zuppke at a time when college football was not only a major sport, but the only type of football that was considered big-time. The civil engineering major starred in both baseball and football, leading the gridiron squad to the Big Ten conference championship in 1918.

After graduating from Illinois, Halas entered the navy during World War I. He was assigned as an ensign at the Great Lakes Naval Training Center, north of Chicago, where he played on a powerful Navy football team, good enough to go to the January 1, 1919, Rose Bowl. There young Halas distinguished himself by catching two touchdown passes and returning an interception 77 yards.

With baseball being the only real major league sport, and Halas's first love, he plied his diamond skills professionally. He played minor league and semipro ball well enough to make the 1919 New York Yankees squad, under Hall of Fame manager Miller Huggins. An outfielder, the 24-year-old Halas appeared in a dozen games, garnering but two hits in 22 at-bats. A hip injury along with other ailments, in addition to being inef-fective in his opportunity with the Yankees, propelled Halas out of baseball for good.

IIe returned to his native Chicago and got a job on the Burlington and Quincy Railroad in the bridge department. Ever the athlete, however, Halas supplemented his $55-a-week earnings by playing weekend football with a team from Hammond, Indiana, composed in part of old Navy teammates. Then, strangely enough, he was recruited. Renowned as a baseball and football star, he was invited by the A. E. Staley Manufacturing Company in Decatur, Illinois, to work in the starch factory, play for their baseball team, and most important, develop a foot-ball team for the Staley Fellowship Club, a program for the company's employees.

The football venture, successful as it was for the Staleys on the grid-iron, with Halas loading his team with "ringers," appeared in jeopardy without a structured league in which to play. Games were often arbitrar-ily canceled when an opponent was offered more money to play another foe, schedules shifted constantly, and some teams simply did not show up for games. As if that were not enough chaos, there were frequent dis-putes over rules.

All this troubled Halas, who also concerned himself with the lack of civility among violently competitive players. "I have made it a team rule that my players behave as gentlemen and dress as gentlemen," he stated while reflecting on his career. "I wanted to end the popular misconcep-tion that professional athletes were a bunch of roughnecks."

Halas then contacted Ralph Hay of the Canton Bulldogs and on September 17, 1920, a meeting of what would become 12 charter fran-chises was held in Canton, and the American Professional Football Association (APFA) was born. Halas, with his love of the gridiron game burning intensely, poured his energies into the formation of the profes-sional football league at a time when the very idea of such an alliance was regarded as folly. Hard work was nothing new to Halas when it came to football. He had not only been player and coach of the Staleys, he even handled ticket sales and other aspects of the business end of the club.

Halas's education in the business side proved valuable. Despite a 10–1–2 championship season in 1920, and other previous success, the Staleys took a financial bath to the tune of $14,406.36, too much for the

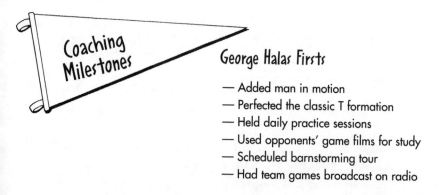

Coaching Milestones

George Halas Firsts

— Added man in motion
— Perfected the classic T formation
— Held daily practice sessions
— Used opponents' game films for study
— Scheduled barnstorming tour
— Had team games broadcast on radio

struggling company to sustain. The Fellowship Club was disbanded and Staley turned the franchise, with $5,000 in seed money, over to Halas. The clever Halas then signed on a business partner, Edward "Dutch" Sternaman, to help bankroll the team.

So it was that Halas turned seeming folly into raging success. Moreover, he is virtually the incarnation of the entire historical evolution of the NFL. His span envelops an era in which teams represented cities so small as to be all but off the mental map of the average fan not living in the state containing them, one in which players played with barely any gear—in some cases without helmets—all the way to the present era in which the Super Bowl has become a near national holiday. His tenure runs from the Massillon, Ohio, Tigers to *Monday Night Football.* He knew everyone from Jim Thorpe to Howard Cosell, from A. E. Staley to Pete Rozelle, from Bronko Nagurski to Walter Payton.

And heart and soul he was. Not only did Halas found the Bears, play for the Bears, own the Bears, and manage the Bears, he coached the Bears—and did so brilliantly.

Look at his record.

In his first tour of duty, Halas went 84–31–19 during the 1920s. He returned in 1933 for yet another decade and won another 84 games against just 22 losses and four ties. Then, after a three-year sabbatical, he donned the whistle for yet another decade, beginning in 1946 and turned in a 75–42–2 record. In 1958, at age 63, he returned yet again for another decade, winning 75 more games with 53 defeats and six stalemates. Four separate tenures and 40 years of coaching—one that began when he was 25 and ended when he was 72, brought (including his 6–3 postseason record) 324 victories, 151 losses, and 31 ties. He won six NFL championships, the first when he was 26 and the last 42 years later in 1963 when he derailed his good friend and intense rival Vince Lombardi's first attempt to win three consecutive NFL championships. He had only six losing seasons.

It then took the Bears 22 years before they could win another NFL crown after Halas left the sideline for good. That one was claimed by the 1985 team, coached by Mike Ditka, who just happened to be the last man directly hired by Halas to coach his beloved Bruins. Until nearly the day Halas died, he faithfully took his seat in the press box area of Soldier Field and cheered loudly, emotionally, and unashamedly for his Bears.

Halas was intelligent, creative, industrious, tough, and compassionate. His intellect made it possible for the Staleys and then the Bears to survive and even thrive. He was an innovator, both on the business side and in his coaching with his use of various formations. It was Halas who, with the help of Clark Shaughnessy of the University of Chicago, introduced the modern version of the T formation in 1940. On the social front, Halas reversed course and became an innovator of a different sort. A man of his era, he had refused to sign black players in the '30s, and Hall of Fame great Fritz Pollard accused Halas of keeping him out of the league in the 1930s

George Halas.

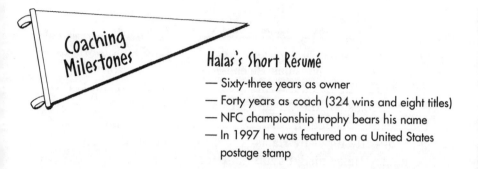

Coaching Milestones

Halas's Short Résumé

— Sixty-three years as owner
— Forty years as coach (324 wins and eight titles)
— NFC championship trophy bears his name
— In 1997 he was featured on a United States postage stamp

and '40s. After the 1948 season, however, Halas drafted the first African American of the modern era, halfback George Taliaferro of Indiana, although Taliaferro never played for the Bears. Halas employed the first black quarterback in '53, one with the apt name of Willie Thrower, from Michigan State.

No one worked harder than Halas, as player-coach to owner-coach into his late sixties. But for him it was fun. "Nothing is work," he was fond of saying, "unless you'd rather be doing something else." Tough on the field, with his checkbook, and especially with his principles—something discovered by George Allen publicly and countless others in private. George Halas was also compassionate. Former players who labored faithfully under his direction earned lifetime loyalty from Halas. No one experienced this more fully than the great Gale Sayers, for whom Halas stood ready to pay any medical bill the running back incurred after his career was over. He gave liberally to charities, often without fanfare, all the while being accused of being miserly.

Halas was the definition of old school. His teams blocked powerfully, tackled ferociously, and no NFL team hit harder than one coached by the man who founded the Bears. A Halas-coached team was competitive and even more than that, it was physical, to the very edge of what the rules permitted. You didn't play for George Halas and fail to invest your last unit of energy on the field. You were there to win, and if you didn't, it was only because the opponent was better. It was not because the opponent gave a better effort.

His was an indomitable will, one that brought out the intense partisanship of rival fans. Halas loved it. "San Francisco has always been my favorite booing city," he once said. "I don't mean the people boo louder or longer, but there is a very special intimacy. When they boo you, you know they mean you. Music, that's what it is to me. One time in Kezar Stadium they gave me a standing boo."

He was a man of traditional values—religion and family chief among them. The staunch Roman Catholic made the Bears a generational franchise, one that included his son, his daughter, his son-in-law, and his grandchildren. The genealogy of the Chicago Bears is the genealogy of George Stanley Halas.

He was an authoritarian, the boss. But it was never about egomania for Halas. Halas was a conservative man, one who believed in a social order in which honesty and integrity were key, and a handshake finalized a deal. He believed in respecting those in authority over him and expected to receive that same respect from those over whom he was the authority. For those who understood and accepted this, few would have a better friend for life than George Halas. For those who did not, there were few more formidable adversaries than the "Old Man."

The Chicago Bears are a single-parent family, and that single parent was George "Papa Bear" Halas. No one loved his human or football family more.

A member of the charter class welcomed into the Pro Football Hall of Fame in 1963, George Halas was not a great figure in the history of the NFL. He was not a giant. He was a colossus, a Goliath. Papa Bear veritably towers over the National Football League in a way no other person has or likely ever will.

DID YOU KNOW . . . That Halas offered to share his team's lucrative television revenues with teams in smaller cities, believing what was good for the league was good for the Bears?

Out of the Gate

A. E. Staley's sponsorship of a professional football team lasted exactly one season. An economic downturn affecting the starch factory after the 1920 season forced his hand, and he encouraged Halas to take over the reins. The young player-coach-entrepreneur did so as owner after the second game of the 1921 season. Sagely, Halas realized his future was in football rather than starch, and perhaps more important, that the future of his franchise lay to the north in the sprawling metropolis of Chicago, rather than in Decatur, Illinois, despite local fan support. That Halas had a plan was a surprise to no one, as planning was foundational to the young football owner.

"Many people flounder about in life because they have no purpose," he once stated. "Before it is possible to achieve anything, an objective must be set." And Halas had an objective. His football dream would become a reality. Things moved forward quickly when Staley's ego and Halas's business acumen combined as the former sponsor paid the new owner the then-princely sum of $5,000 to keep the name "Staleys" for one more year.

Halas had still another hurdle to negotiate before moving the team. He needed permission from Chris O'Brien, owner of the Racine (named after a Chicago street) Cardinals, to do business in the Windy City because O'Brien held territorial rights to the "city of the big shoulders." Upon receiving it, Halas worked out an arrangement with William Veeck Sr., owner of the Chicago Cubs, to play Staley games at Cub Park (later named Wrigley Field) in exchange for 15 percent of the gross receipts. Halas saved some precious dollars by offering former Illinois classmate and Staley player Dutch Sternaman a half-ownership in lieu of a salary.

As for the team, Halas was able to bring two stellar performers, Guy Chamberlin and George Trafton, to Chicago to continue playing for the Staleys. Halas had the touch, as he and the Staleys got out of the gate with a 10–1–1 record, winning the APFA championship. It was no small accomplishment, as the league had 13 members. It was also a disputed one. Second-place Buffalo (9–1–2) protested the title, claiming that Chicago's record included nonleague games, but Joe F. Carr, a Columbus, Ohio, sportswriter who had taken over as league president, ruled in favor of Halas and the Staleys. The 1921 season was also the first year of a rival franchise that would become very important in Chicago Staley-Bear football history, the Acme Packers from Green Bay, Wisconsin, coached by Earl "Curly" Lambeau. The Packers finished fourth with a 6–2–2 record.

Ever the innovator, Halas suggested the American Professional Football Association change its cumbersome name to the National

Wrigley Field, shown here hosting the 1937 NFL championship game between the Bears and Washington Redskins, served as the Bears home for 50 years.

That Curly Lambeau repaid the generosity of Don Murphy in a most unusual way? He allowed Murphy—a civilian by football standards—to start the opening game of the season and play one minute of NFL football as a reward for his generosity.

Football League, a name that became the league's official moniker for the 1922 campaign. As for his own team, on January 28 Halas renamed them the Chicago Bears, linking the team's football identity to that of the popular Chicago Cubs, whose park his team called home.

The NFL was hardly big league in the early '20s. Teams hailed from such comparatively small Ohio towns as Canton, Toledo, Dayton, Akron, and Marion. In addition there were teams in Hammond and Evansville (Indiana), Rock Island (Illinois), Kenosha (Wisconsin), and Duluth (Minnesota). And one of the quirks of the league was that laws forbid Sunday play in some cities, resulting in teams playing at home on Saturday and on the road a day later, giving new meaning to the term *back-to-back.*

The '22 season also marked the team's first "trade." Troubled that his team could not block the Rock Island Independents' great lineman, Ed Healey, Halas paid the Rock Island team $100 for the gridiron great's contract. Healey was excited about the trade, chiefly because of the upgrade in facilities. Rock Island had neither a trainer nor a shower room. "At Wrigley Field we had a nice warm place to dress and nice warm showers," said the Bears great.

Two shutouts at the hands of the crosstown Cardinals, 6–0 and 9–0, were costly as the 9–3 Bears finished second in the then 18-team NFL to the renowned Bulldogs of Canton. It was a bitter outcome as the 10–0–2 Bulldogs were led by player-coach Guy Chamberlin, who left Halas for greater professional opportunities.

The forceful President Carr tightened up NFL procedures in 1922, disciplining the Green Bay franchise for employing college athletes under assumed names. Carr returned the team's $50 entry fee and threw the Acme Packers out of the NFL. An alarmed and chastened Curly Lambeau shelled out $50 from his own pocket to buy back the franchise and restore it to the league. His friend Don Murphy sold a car to raise train fare for the frantic Lambeau so that Curly could attend the league meeting. After vowing to adhere to the rules, Carr readmitted Green Bay to the NFL.

Cash was the mother's milk of the NFL franchises, and the Bears managed to eke out a $1,476.92 profit in 1922 after the final checks were mailed. Whether as businessman or coach, George Halas was a winner.

The '23 season was in many respects a replay of 1922, with the Bears posting a strong 9–2–2 log, but not as strong as Canton's undefeated 11–0–1 in the then 20-team NFL. The season outcome was particularly bitter for Halas because the Bulldogs were led by none other than player-coach Guy Chamberlin. It was more of the same a year later. The Bears, after losing to the Bulldogs in their second game, went on to an otherwise undefeated 6–1–4 season, again second to the Bulldogs who posted a 7–1–1 mark in their new venue, 55 miles north in Cleveland.

TRIVIA

The star player of the arch-rival Cardinals was John "Paddy" Driscoll. Which NFL team did he later coach?

Answers to the trivia questions are on pages 182–183.

One of Halas's highlights in 1923 involved the great Jim Thorpe. In 1922 Thorpe and other Native American players formed a new team called the Oorang Indians, playing their games in Marion, Ohio. The Bears player-coach picked up a Thorpe fumble on the Chicago 2-yard line and raced 98 yards for a score. It was a most uncomfortable scamper. "I could feel Thorpe breathing down my neck all the way," said Halas.

Though a three-time bridesmaid on the gridiron, the Bears' bank account was the envy of many around the league. Indeed, pro football was taking root on Chicago's North Side as Halas and Sternaman divided an outrageous $20,000 in profits at the close of the 1924 season.

No Cigars

The professional game was struggling in the middle '20s. Teams were routinely in the red, with some folding. Moreover, professional football players were most certainly not celebrities, but rather regarded as former athletes unable to find more respectable employment. While pro football struggled, college football thrived. Games were played before packed stadiums, and the college stars were national heroes.

Against that backdrop George Halas made an incredibly bold move. Seeing the need for a force that would energize pro football in general and his beloved Bears in particular, the owner acquired the services of the most celebrated of all college players, the great Harold "Red" Grange in November of 1925, after he concluded his career at Illinois. Grange was such hot gridiron property that he was arguably the first real media figure as an NFL football player. Grange, realizing his celebrity, actually had a manager, C. C. Pyle, (what would be called an agent today) work out his deal with the Bears and other profitable uses of his celebrity. The bringing in of a college player before he graduated was itself a thunderbolt to the football world, but Halas and the Bears took it a rather bold step further and went on a barnstorming tour with Grange during the winter to gain notoriety for the Bears and more than a few dollars for the team (and Grange).

Grange paid a price for opting to play professionally for the Bears. "It [the decision to jump to pro football] wasn't all that easy, though," recalled Grange years later. "Most of the college coaches and a lot of the sportswriters were very down on it. 'Football isn't meant to be played for money, Zup [Bob Zuppke, Grange's college coach at Illinois] said to me'...I told Zup, 'You get paid for coaching it. Why should it be wrong for me to get paid for playing it?' No matter what, he was still opposed to it, and we didn't really talk to each other for a number of years after I agreed to play with the pros."

Nonetheless, Grange and the Bears drew more than 36,000 fans to their Thanksgiving Day game against the rival Cardinals. The elusive Grange was a spectacular punt returner, but Cardinals star John "Paddy" Driscoll cleverly punted away from Grange all day, much to the displeasure of the booing crowd who were anxiously awaiting one of the Galloping Ghost's vintage runbacks. The size of the crowd was perhaps the highlight of the afternoon, as the Cardinals held Grange to but 36 yards as they battled the Bruins to a 0–0 tie. "Kicking to Grange," Driscoll said before the game, "is like grooving one to Babe Ruth." After the game was over and Grange had made his uneventful debut, Driscoll stopped at the seats

Red Grange, here with his University of Illinois coach Bob Zuppke. Zuppke was opposed to Grange playing football professionally.

1920s Bears Greats

Backs and Receivers

George Halas, End—A both-ways star.

Guy Chamberlin, End—Chamberlin played only two years for the Staleys but was an outstanding 60-minute man at end and a stone winner. He enjoyed a sparkling 58–16–7 record as an NFL coach. In five of his six coaching seasons, Chamberlin also played.

Paddy Driscoll, Running Back—Driscoll came over from the Cardinals, who were paying him the handsome sum of $300 a game. The 5'11", 160-pound Driscoll was a six-time All-NFL player.

behind the Cardinals bench to chat with his wife. The crowd started booing, prompting Driscoll to remark to his wife, "I hate to hear fans boo a young man like Grange. It wasn't his fault he couldn't break one today."

"Don't feel sorry for Grange," his wife said. "It's you they're booing."

The hated Cardinals finished the NFL season with an 11–2–1 mark; the Bears finished a solid but not outstanding 9–5–3. The Bears played 19 games on the barnstorming circuit, finishing with a 13–5–1 record.

In 1926 Grange's manager, C. C. Pyle, approached Halas for a five-figure salary and one-third ownership of the Bears for his client. That Halas would have none of such a presumptuous request could not have been a surprise to Pyle, who wanted to bring an NFL franchise to New York. With the deal quashed, Pyle formed his own team, the New York Yankees, with Grange as its centerpiece hoping to have it accepted into the NFL. When he failed to persuade the league to admit his new team, Pyle, in his own way as stubborn as Halas, formed a rival league called the American Football League for his new team, thinking that with Grange as the poster boy for the highlighted New York franchise, the league might survive.

It didn't, sputtering through the 1926 season and breathing its last before entering a second campaign. All was not lost for Pyle and Grange, however, as the Yankees were annexed by the NFL. For Grange 1927 was not a banner year. He severely injured his knee in the third game of the season, against the Bears no less, forever robbing him of his blinding speed.

When drawing-card Grange and the Bears parted company in 1926 over a business and salary dispute, the enterprising Halas scrambled to acquire Cardinals star Driscoll from the financially strapped archrivals across town for $13,500. With that, the Bears were more than ready to contend for the NFL crown. It came down to a confrontation between Chicago and the Frankford Yellow Jackets. In a fiercely contested game, the 13-1-1 Yellow Jackets emerged with a 7-6 victory over the 12-0-3 Bears on the strength of a blocked Driscoll extra point—stuffed by none other than Guy Chamberlin, who had moved on to Frankford to become the team's player-coach.

The next two years were successful but not champagne-drinking years, as the Bears posted 9-3-2 and 7-5-1 records. The 1928 season was marred by a power struggle between the combative Halas and his

1920s Bears Greats

Linemen

Ed Healey, Tackle—Out of Dartmouth, Healey was an all-league pick five times and often called the most versatile tackle ever, possessing great speed for a lineman.

George Trafton, Center—With the exception of 1922 when he took a year off to coach at Northwestern, Trafton was with Halas from 1920 to 1932. Known for extraordinary combativeness and called "the meanest, toughest player alive" by Red Grange, Trafton was an all-star six times.

Link Lyman, Tackle—After joining the Bears on the 1925 barnstorming tour, Lyman remained with the team for the duration of his career. Lyman was renowned for shifting in the defensive line to confuse offensive blockers. He experienced only one losing season throughout his entire high school, college (Nebraska), and professional career—one that spanned 16 seasons.

partner Dutch Sternaman over who would run the offense, a tiff that may have contributed to the team's fifth-place finish.

When Red Grange emerged from retirement to join the Bears in '29, hopes were high. The team bolted to a 4–1–1 log early, but although still a solid back, Grange's mobility was hampered by his bad knee, and the team closed the season in reverse, dropping eight of its final nine and ending the year with a first-ever losing record of 4–9–2. The 1929 season was especially distasteful to Halas because their hated rivals to the north, the Green Bay Packers, took their first NFL title that year.

Halas and his Bears had begun the Roaring '20s with a menacing growl, but closed the decade on the downside. From 1926 on, the trend was clearly and disturbingly downward. After a strong 12–1–3 '26, the team slipped to a respectable 9–3–2 in 1927. That was followed by another slide to 7–5–1 in '28, and then an unthinkable 4–9–2 at the decade's end. In three short years the Bears had gone from 12-game winners to a team that could boast but four victories.

The Galloping Ghost

Born in Forksville, Pennsylvania, on June 13, 1903, Harold "Red" Grange was the Babe Ruth of the gridiron. Grange's mother died when he was five. His father, Lyle, moved the family to Wheaton, Illinois, where he worked his way up to police chief, while young Red became a high school sports prodigy. After winning 16 letters in high school, Grange—quite amazingly—did not think he was good enough to play at the University of Illinois when he entered there in 1922. This despite scoring 75 touchdowns and tallying 532 points at Wheaton High School. His frat brothers thought differently and persuaded the reluctant warrior to give it a try.

Grange made the team in spades. He scored two TDs in a scrimmage against the varsity, one a 60-yard jaunt. Wearing No. 77, by his sophomore year he was a near-icon to college football adherents, scoring three touchdowns on runs of 12, 35, and 60 yards in his first varsity game. He picked off opponent's passes, ran from scrimmage, and led the Western Conference (later the Big Ten) in scoring en route to being named All-American.

In 1924 Grange faced what would be his sternest test so far, a game against the vaunted Wolverines of Michigan. The Michigan squad was unbeaten in 20 straight games, leading athletics director and former coach Fielding Yost to boast, "Mr. Grange will be carefully watched every time he takes the ball. There will be 11 clean, hard Michigan tacklers headed for him."

The Wolverines needed more than 11, as Grange scored touchdowns the first four times he got his hands on the ball. The spectacular performance included a 95-yard kickoff return, and then 67-, 56-, and 45-yard runs from scrimmage. He scored again in the third quarter and even fired a touchdown pass as the Illini buried Michigan, 39–14. Later injured and missing the final game of the season, Grange was again an All-American.

So celebrated was the youth that he had acquired many nicknames, including "The Illinois Flash" and the most famous, "The Galloping Ghost." His was the golden age of college football, a time when sportswriters rhapsodized over heroics on the gridiron. After the Michigan game, the great Grantland Rice gave Grange his nickname, writing:

A Streak of fire, a breath of flame
Eluding all who reach and clutch;
A gray ghost thrown into the game
That rival hands may never touch;
A rubber bounding, blasting soul
Whose destination is the goal.

Red Grange takes a break during a game against the New York Giants in 1925.

"This man Red Grange of Illinois is three or four men rolled into one football player," enthused the great Damon Runyon. "He is Jack Dempsey, Babe Ruth, Al Jolson, Paavo Nurmi, and Man o' War. Put together, they spell Grange."

TRIVIA

In the 1920s, Grange, in addition to two films, made a movie serial. What was its title?

Answers to the trivia questions are on pages 182–183.

As for the 5'11", 175-pound Grange, football was far simpler. "If you have the football and 11 guys are after you," he reasoned aloud, "if you're smart, you'll run." In his senior year, with Illinois dropping three of its first four games, he was moved to quarterback and the 1925 squad closed the campaign with four straight triumphs. Grange rolled up 363 yards and three touchdowns in a win against Pennsylvania before 65,000 awed rooters.

Unlike today, college football players rarely extended their careers in the professional leagues upon graduating, the pros being considered a second-class football entity populated by toothless ruffians unable to find more-dignified work. George Halas and the NFL, however, needed a boost, particularly at the gate, so he and partner Dutch Sternaman ruminated over how much of a lift the addition of the Galloping Ghost would provide. Deciding it would be substantial, the two signed Grange to a peculiar agreement, one that had the Ghost back on the gridiron almost immediately after his college career was concluded.

Having signed a personal services contract for a whopping $100,000 with promoter Charles C. "Cash and Carry" Pyle, who then sold the athlete's services to the Bears, Grange hardly had time to catch his football breath, as the three-time All-American left college to go on a 19-game, 67-day, coast-to-cost barnstorming tour with George Halas's Chicago Bears. Grange was to receive $3,000 per game and a percentage of the gate from Halas.

Leaving college to go pro instantly was an unheard-of breach of protocol at the time. "I'd have been more popular with the colleges if I had joined Capone's mob in Chicago, rather than the Bears," Grange recounted.

The tour, part regular-season games and part exhibitions, began with an incredible 10 games in 18 days in the Midwest. After a two-week respite the team would head south and west for nine more contests. For Grange the tour fell short of expectations. He got hurt, missing several

DID YOU KNOW . . . That Grange claimed to know that it was time for him to retire when in a January 27, 1935, postseason exhibition game, he broke free on a 50-yard run only to be tackled from behind by, of all players, a lineman?

games and playing sparingly in others. It was a go at the cashbox, however, as 36,600 fans shunned their turkeys and jammed their way into Wrigley Field on Thanksgiving Day when he made his Chicago debut, a day in which Halas was reported to have wept as he counted the receipts. The archrival Cardinals, kicking away from Grange on punts, hung tough for a 0–0 tie. Another 65,000 curious fans turned out in New York, easily the largest assemblage to see a professional football game in the Big Apple up to that time. Grange then broke that standard in January when 75,000 came out to see him in Los Angeles. Ever the hustler, Pyle procured a movie role for his client (*One Minute to Play*), a vaudeville tour, and two other movie spots. Grange lapped up the luxury, returning to Wheaton at the end of the tour driving a $5,500 Lincoln and sporting a $500 raccoon coat.

Pyle wanted a piece (one-third) of the Bears as part of a 1926 agreement with Grange, but was rebuffed by Halas. From there the Pyle-Grange duo went on to form the New York Yankees football team, partially realizing a dream of Pyle's to bring an NFL football franchise to the nation's largest city. The NFL, however, put up a no-entry sign. Undaunted, Pyle started the ill-fated American Football League with Grange the featured star of the New York Yankees. The league limped through the 1926 season, and the Yankees were absorbed into the NFL for the '27 season when the fledgling league folded.

In an ironic twist, Grange sustained a severe knee injury early in the '27 season against the Bears and was simply never the same electrifying runner again. After missing the entire 1928 season, in another turn of fate Grange signed with the Bears and resumed his playing career under Halas. No longer the scintillating runner he had been in his glory years, the versatile Grange became a defensive standout in an era of one-platoon football. He was named to the first-ever All-Pro team in 1931 and repeated the honor in 1932. He concluded his career after the 1934 season.

After his football career Grange continued to capitalize on his celebrity. First he made a living in the insurance business and then found his way into the broadcasting booth. He was the analyst on the Bears games for 14 seasons until 1963, after which he moved to network television for college games.

Upon later life reflection, the Ghost, who was a charter member of both the Pro and College Football Halls of Fame, kept his football exploits in perspective. "They built my accomplishments way out of proportion," he said. "I never got the idea that I was a tremendous big shot. I could carry a football well, but there are a lot of doctors and teachers and engineers who could do their thing better than I."

In 1991 he died of pneumonia in Lake Wales, Florida. He was 87.

A New Sheriff in Town

With the team less successful than either he or partner Dutch Sternaman wished, and with them vying over how the offense should be run, Halas effected a compromise with his then somewhat alienated partner and agreed to hire former Illinois assistant and current Lake Forest Academy coach Ralph Jones to take over as head coach.

The new sheriff was his own man. After promising a championship in three years upon being hired, the new coach went to work on altering the offense. He moved the ends out wide, moved the halfbacks further apart, and put one of them in motion. This offered great flexibility, because in addition to being a runner, the man in motion could move downfield for a pass, or cut over and block the defensive end on a run. Off the field, Halas was active. With Driscoll retiring, he signed the 6'2", 230-pound fullback Bronko Nagurski out of Minnesota and fellow fullback Joe Savoldi out of Notre Dame. The league fined the Bears $1,000 because Savoldi hadn't graduated with his class, a fine the Bears grudgingly paid.

Jones's efforts paid off, as he restored the team to its winning ways, posting a 9–4–1 record.

At the conclusion of the 1930 season Halas helped arrange a December 30 exhibition game between the Bears and the crosstown Cardinals. What made it novel is that the game was played indoors, at the Chicago Stadium. One of the purposes of the event was to aid unemployed people suffering from the Great Depression. The Bears prevailed on the 80-yard field 9–7 before 10,000 fans.

The following season was a near replay of 1930, as the team was 8–5. A high point of the year was the naming of the first All-Pro team. Red Grange was the only Bear selected.

That another rival league was formed in 1936, also calling itself the American Football League? The league lasted two seasons. Its original members were the champion Boston Shamrocks, Brooklyn Tigers, Cleveland Rams, New York Yankees, Pittsburgh Americans, and the Brooklyn Rochester Tigers. In its second and final season, the title went to the Los Angeles Bulldogs.

By 1932 it was time for Jones to make good on his three-year championship promise. Halas signed a star, end Bill Hewitt out of Michigan, who didn't wear a helmet, and the Bears went into the final game of the season matched against hated Green Bay needing to win to be in the championship hunt. The Bruins won a grudging battle, 9–0, with Bronko Nagurski providing the only touchdown on a 56-yard rumble. The win gave Chicago a curious 7–1–6 mark and an opportunity to play the Portsmouth (Ohio) Spartans for the title.

Subzero temperatures on that December 18 day forced Halas to move the game inside. It was played on an 80-yard "field" in the Chicago Stadium. A loud throng of 11,198 fans watched a taut contest. Nagurski took a fourth-down handoff on the 2 and headed for the goal line. He stunned the Spartans by stopping abruptly and lofting a TD aerial to Grange, alone in the end zone, helping the Bears to a 9–0 win.

Jones was an honest man, the Bears were champions again, and the team lost $18,000, causing Sternaman to sell his share of the team to Halas. Halas bought him out for $38,000, borrowing the money to do so.

In 1933 the 10-team league split into Eastern and Western divisions, with the Bears in the West. Jones resigned a champion, returning to Lake Forest Academy as football coach and athletics director. Halas, in part to defray costs, returned to the sideline as head coach. Halas was deadly serious about making his team a force, holding the first-ever out-of-town training camp at Notre Dame. The team rolled to a 10–2–1 mark en route to the league's first-ever NFL championship game. The contest pitted the Bears against the Giants before 26,000 hooting fans in Wrigley Field. The fans were well entertained as the two teams scrapped evenly with the Bears holding a razor-thin 23–21 advantage in the fourth quarter, much on the strength of rookie kicker Jack Manders's 11 points.

In the game's final moments, however, New York wingback Dale Burnett broke into the clear, heading straight for the end zone, with only Grange—who had registered the only score in the '32 title game—in his way. It was not as easy as merely tackling Burnett, as the runner was trailed by center Mel Hein to whom Burnett could lateral if Grange made contact. The Ghost exhibited his Hall of Fame savvy by seizing Burnett around the chest, and in so doing preventing him from pitching the ball to Hein. The two were rolling on the turf as the gun went off, giving the Bears their second consecutive title.

The game featured some Bears razzle-dazzle as well. Nagurski set up the winning points when he lobbed a short throw to Hewitt, who in turn lateraled the ball to Bill Karr, who scored a 36-yard TD.

The 1934 season opened with yet another football innovation, the College All-Star Game, to be played annually between the reigning NFL champion and the best of the previous year's college crop in Soldier Field at the end of August. The game was significant, marking a bit of an alliance between the NFL and the college game. Sponsored by the Chicago Tribune Charities, the Bears left their Lane Tech High School (Chicago) training camp and took on the All-Stars before 79,432 fans on August 31, battling to a scoreless tie.

The big addition to the Chicago roster in '34 was running back Beattie Feathers, from Tennessee. The rookie became the first pro to rush for 1,000 yards, racking up 1,004 as the Bears roared to a 13–0 season. He averaged an incredible 9.94 yards per carry, much due to the punishing blocking of teammate Nagurski, who came in fourth with 586 yards of his own on 22 more attempts than Feathers.

The Bears—who averaged exactly 22 points per game, easily leading the NFL on offense—yielded only 86 points in their 13 games, an average of just 6.6 a game. One other team did better. The 10–3 Detroit Lions gave up only 59 points.

DID YOU KNOW . . . That when Halas bought partner Sternaman out, he borrowed $5,000 from none other than team vice president Charles Bidwell, who would own the archrival Cardinals a year later?

Bronko Nagurski (right) and Red Grange both played for the Bears after celebrated college careers. They helped make Chicago the capital of pro football during its emerging years.

On December 9 the Bears traveled to New York's Polo Grounds for an NFL title rematch with the Giants, who had gone a mediocre 8–5 by comparison, scoring barely more than half (147) the number of points as the potent Bears (286).

The Bears held a 10–3 halftime lead on a slippery, frozen New York field. At the half, some of the Giants switched to basketball shoes to gain footing on the icy tundra. It worked. Trailing 13–3 going into the fourth quarter, the New Yorkers exploded for 27 points to win going away, 30–13, and robbing the Chicagoans of a perfect season, and more important, a coveted third straight NFL championship. The loss, in what became known as "The Sneaker Game," became more bitter when, in the following season, the Bears dropped to a 6–4–2 record in part due to injuries to Nagurski and Feathers.

TRIVIA

Which famous player did the Bears select in 1936, upon gaining rights to him from the Philadelphia Eagles, but who never played for Chicago?

Answers to the trivia questions are on pages 182–183.

The NFL was picking up steam by 1936, the year of the first college draft, one in which the player limit was expanded to 25. On the advice of West Virginians Bill Karr and quarterback Carl Brumbaugh, Halas tabbed tackle Joe Stydahar from their native state university and selected Colgate guard Danny Fortmann as well. Nagurski returned from his injuries, and Manders led the league in field goals as the Bears posted a 9–3–0 mark, finishing second to the hated Green Bay Packers in the West. The Pack went on to defeat Washington for the NFL championship.

Hard Men

Professional football in the early years was a violent sport, filled with brawling brutes who loved to mix it up with opposing players. In fact, the hooliganism typical of some of the most unrefined participants contributed heavily to the negative stereotype much of the public had of the sport. Whereas today, college stars will eagerly forego some of their eligibility if they can make it in the NFL, in earlier times playing pro football held little positive status. College stars routinely put their diplomas to good use in the business and professional, white-collar worlds, rather than stoop to playing in the blue-collar NFL, amid "illiterate bullies" who gloried in the physical contact of the game. The Bears had their share of tough guys over the years, but few were tougher than George Trafton, Bill Hewitt, and Bronko Nagurski.

Trafton, who turned pro after a single year at Notre Dame after being expelled by Knute Rockne for playing semipro football, had no peer as a hard-hitting center for the Bears from 1920 to 1932. The length of Trafton's career was uncharacteristic of the time. The 6'2" 235-pounder was the first center to snap the ball with one hand, was named to All-Pro teams six times, and was regarded as the top center of the 1920s. He was colorful and brawling, willing to engage in "dirty" tactics, and renowned for mixing it up with opponents in on-field rumbles. He reveled in his image and gloried in being unpopular in rival towns, prompting one observer to claim that Trafton was strongly disliked in every NFL city except two, Green Bay and Rock Island. There he was hated.

Trafton, nicknamed appropriately "The Brute," was once charged with putting out four Rock Island players in 12 plays, causing the Rock Island squad to assign a hatchet man to him when they played again. The would-be enforcer was carried off the field, and legend has it that one could see the imprint of cleats from his forehead down to his chin. Once after breaking the leg of a Rock Island ballcarrier, Trafton raced for the nearest exit at game's end. After hurrying out of the park and into a cab, a pack of incensed local fans threw rocks against the vehicle's windows, forcing Trafton to race down the highway with the fans in hot pursuit before hitching a ride from an unsuspecting motorist.

Halas, aware of Trafton's notoriety in Rock Island, once turned the team's share of the gate, $7,000, to Trafton's safekeeping. "I knew that if trouble came," said Halas, "Trafton would be running for his life. I would only be running for $7,000."

Bronko Nagurski, here in 1943, retired in the 1930s then returned to the Bears during World War II.

Labeled as a tough, mean, and ornery critter by Grange, the Packers' press book offered its take on Trafton when he joined the Pack as a line coach in 1944. "Green Bay fans never liked Trafton when he was with the Bears, because they saw him as a truculent, blustery competitor who tried to arouse their contempt."

TRIVIA

What was Bill Hewitt's nick-name to Bears fans, who were regaled by his quick-ness? What did his teammates call him?

Answers to the trivia questions are on pages 182–183.

The 5'9", 170-pound Hewitt joined the Bears in 1932 from the University of Michigan. He was a two-way end who had immediate impact in the '32 championship season. He had very long and exceptionally strong arms and used them to "shiver" blockers and stop ballcarriers. Averaging 50 minutes a game, Hewitt was an amazingly quick, big-play performer who constantly developed gimmicks to fool opponents. He was All-Pro six times, the last two with the Philadelphia Eagles, making him the first to be named All-Pro for more than one team.

Hewitt was a great player who died young at 37. He was also a tough player, cast in the take-no-prisoners Bears image. He was once described as three parts gorilla and one part Englishman. Despite the incredible violence of the game, Hewitt refused to wear a helmet—not for just one year, but for his entire career. He donned his first headgear in 1939 when NFL rules mandated it.

Indeed, many coaches discouraged the wearing of helmets at this time. In 1912 the legendary Glenn "Pop" Warner, coach of the Jim Thorpe–led Carlisle Indians, made this bizarre statement: "Playing without helmets gives players more confidence, saves their heads from many hard jolts, and keeps their ears from becoming torn or sore. I do not encourage their use. I have never seen an accident to the head which was serious, but I have many times seen cases when hard bumps on the head so dazed the player receiving them that he lost his memory for a time and had to be removed from the game."

More famous than Hewitt was one Bronislaw Nagurski (Bronko's family were immigrants from Polish Ukraine), a fullback out of Minnesota. Nagurski was a human bulldozer who symbolized the power of the pro game. Many felt that Nagurski simply had no equal when it came to straight-ahead line-smashing running. His blocking and tackling were equally ferocious. Nagurski was simply overpowering. In an era in which tackles played at 175 to 190 pounds, the 6'2", 228-pound Nagurski was a crushing force. He had a 19½ ring size and a 19-inch neck.

So effective and intimidating was Nagurski that Dick Richards, owner of the Detroit Lions, once approached the "Bronk" before a game and said, "Here's a check for $10,000, Nagurski. Not for playing with the Lions, because you belong to the Bears, but just to quit and get the hell out of the league. You're ruining my team."

George Halas liked to tell another story about Nagurski's zeal. In a game at Wrigley Field, which was designed for baseball and had a wall very close to one of the end zones, Nagurski scored a touchdown from the 2-yard line after bulldozing his way through two defenders. With his head still down and his legs churning, Nagurski continued full-steam ahead until he collided with the wall at the back of the end zone, which finally brought him down. He promptly leaped to his feet and returned to the sideline, remarking to a stunned Halas, "That last guy really gave me a good lick, Coach."

The estimable Grantland Rice described collegiate Nagurski by saying, "He was a star end, a star tackle, and a crushing fullback who could pass. Eleven Nagurskis would be a mop-up. It would be something close to murder and massacre." As a professional, in a game at Wrigley Field, Nagurski broke a defender's shoulder, knocked another would-be tackler out, and then slammed into a brick wall, cracking it as he scored the winning touchdown.

His play with the Bears was simply breathtaking, as the monstrous Nagurski was named All-Pro in seven of his eight seasons.

The Bears had many NFL tough guys, but these three Hall of Famers, George Trafton, Bill Hewitt, and Bronko Nagurski, contributed heavily to the hard-nosed reputation of the Chicago Bears.

Closing Out the '30s

Four years removed from their last NFL title, Halas was anxious to return to the top of the pro football world in 1937. Hoping to capitalize on their defense that had yielded but 94 points in their 9–3 campaign in '36, the Bears had to climb over the archrival Packers to claim the Western Division title.

The Packers proved formidable, but the Bears fought their way to a 9–1–1 record, ahead of the 7–4 Pack. They did so actually scoring fewer points and yielding more than the year before, and splitting their two games with Green Bay. Two topflight newcomers, ends George Wilson and former Eagles star Eggs Manske, bolstered the squad. They, along with All-Pros George Musso and Danny Fortmann, helped take the team to the championship game against Washington.

Musso, the Bears' inspirational leader, played against two United States presidents. While at Millikin he played opposite Ron "Dutch" Reagan, a guard at Illinois' Eureka College, and later lined up against Michigan's Gerald Ford in the College All-Star Game. Out of tiny Millikin, Musso was not hotly sought after, so when Halas offered him a tryout, he presented the following financial package. Musso would get $90 per game if he made the team, and for coming up from Decatur to try out, Musso received $5 in expenses, $3 for his train ticket, and $2 more for incidentals. Obviously, Musso made the team.

According to legend, Halas drafted the seemingly too small 6'0", 200-pound Danny Fortmann with his final 1936 pick because he liked his name. The cerebral Fortmann was a Phi Beta Kappa scholar at Colgate and graduated from the University of Chicago Medical School in 1940 while playing for the Bears. He became one of the nation's top orthopedic surgeons. Fortmann also played football with "surgical" skill. His

TRIVIA

Which position did Sid Luckman play as a 1939 rookie?

Answers to the trivia questions are on pages 182–183.

college coach, Andy Kerr, calling Fortmann the best player he ever coached, said Fortmann "blocked with the sureness of a chopping axe. With his keen sense of play development, he always seemed to turn up where he could be most effective."

Musso, Fortmann, and two other All-Pros, Joe Stydahar (who stood 6' 4" tall and weighed 233 pounds and was the Bears' first-ever draft pick in 1936) and Frank Bausch, led the Bears in the championship game in front of 15,870 spectators at Wrigley Field. At quarterback for Washington was the incomparable Sammy Baugh in his first season out of Texas Christian. Slingin' Sammy led the league in passing, hitting on 81 of 171 passes for 1,127 yards and eight TDs during the campaign. The Bears figured to win this tussle, because the 8–3 Washington squad had scored fewer points and yielded more than the Bears, who would be playing the game in their Wrigley Field lair.

In frosty, near-zero weather the great Sammy Baugh hit on 17 of 34 passes for an unheard-of 347 yards to guide his team to a 28–21 win over the Bears. Each Bear received a check for $127.78 as his share for playing the championship contest, and Nagurski retired.

Beattie Feathers, who was never able to equal his glorious rookie season, was traded to Brooklyn before the 1938 season, and Halas acquired fullback Joe Maniaci from the Brooklyn Dodgers. On the field, the team took a giant step backward, winning but six of its 11 games, as Green Bay reclaimed the Western Division crown with an 8–3 log.

The team roared back in '39, however, winning four of its first five games. Their only loss was to fellow Western Division contender, the despised Green Bay Packers, by a thin 21–16 count in Wisconsin. The Bears dropped to 4–3 after losing a cliff-hanger in New York, 16–13, and being shut out at home by the Lions, 10–0. The gloom lifted the

DID YOU KNOW . . . That Baugh had such impact on the game that the rules were changed? Baugh was often subjected to roughhouse tactics in efforts to quell his passing acumen, so the league enacted a 15-yard penalty for roughing the passer.

Consistently great, these Bears, here in 1940, helped lead Chicago to numerous championship games in the prewar years. On the line from left: George Wilson, right end; Lee Artoe, tackle; George Musso, guard; Clyde Turner, center; Dan Fortmann, guard; Joe Stydahar, tackle; and Bob Nowaskey, left end. In the backfield from left: George McAfee, halfback; Bill Osmanski, fullback; Sid Luckman, quarterback; and Ray Nolting, halfback.

following week, however, when the Bruins won a 30–27 verdict from Green Bay. Although they swept their remaining three encounters, the midseason swoon cost them the West, as the Packers finished one game in front with a 9–2 record. The second-place finish was especially galling, as the Bears outscored their opponents by 141 points, 61 more than champion Green Bay.

The '39 season involved more than a turnaround in the Bears' record. The team's T formation was increasing in complexity as new plays were developed. A seminal figure in this architecture was Clark Shaughnessy, a volunteer assistant coach. The quarterback became a key ball handler in the evolving offense, and Halas drafted Sid Luckman out of Columbia, believing the signal caller would be able to master the system. He also drafted fullback Bill Osmanski from Holy Cross. The Osmanski pick proved immediately fruitful as the rookie led the league in rushing with 699 yards. Maniaci was third with 544. The constant tinkering with the

1930s Bears Greats

Bronko Nagurski, Fullback—According to many, the giant from Paul Bunyan country was the most dominating player in the NFL during his time in the game.

Bill Hewitt, End—Hewitt was simply an all-around star. Extremely strong with long arms, the All-Pro end bedeviled offenses with his quickness and defenses with his big plays.

George Musso, Guard—Out of tiny Millikin College in Decatur, Illinois, once the home of the Decatur Staleys, the 6'2", 262-pound Musso was the team captain for nine years. Musso started as a tackle but excelled as a middle guard on defense and a pulling guard on offense and was the first player to be All-NFL at two positions.

Danny Fortmann, Guard—Drafted at 19, Fortmann, who joined the team in 1936, played well into the '40s. Receiving All-NFL honors for eight years, Fortmann called signals for the offensive linemen.

offense paid huge dividends in '39, as the Bears exploded for 298 points, 56 more than runner-up Washington. The defense did not keep pace, however, giving up 157.

On a sad note, NFL president Joe Carr died in May 1939. The former Columbus newspaperman had taken over for Jim Thorpe in 1921 and been the man in charge for 19 years. Carr had accomplished what he had been called to do: make order out of chaos. It was under Carr that the league became the NFL in 1922 and stabilized its franchises such that by the end of the '30s the NFL had a sound identity. It was Carr who ended the unsavory practice of college ringers playing under assumed names in the NFL and owners employing collegians before their graduation date—something Halas did with Grange for great profit. Carr also instituted the first standard player's contract, putting to an end backroom bamboozling and private deals. A tough-minded, clear-thinking man, unafraid of making decisions, carved out a solid reputation as a sports executive such that he also assisted minor league baseball and professional basketball as well. Carr, just 59 at his death, had loomed large and would be missed. League secretary-treasurer Carl Storck would take over as acting president.

As for the Bears, the decade closed in a bittersweet fashion. The team had spiked upward, but not enough to claim the division championship. Overall it had been a solid decade, with four first-place finishes and two NFL titles. The team won 85 games during the '30s, losing just 28 and tying 11. The '30s win total was one more than that of the previous decade, when the team went 84–31–19. Now 110 games over .500 in their first two decades of existence, the Monsters of the Midway readied themselves for what they hoped would be the team's greatest decade ever.

The Hated Packers

The Packers-Bears rivalry actually began off the field in 1921. That was the year two young coaches, George Halas and Curly Lambeau, got a taste of each other's zeal. It was also the year when the Packers were put out of the league for using a college player before his class had graduated.

Indeed the Packers were guilty, but most of the teams engaged in this practice, covering it up by having the players use fictitious names. There was also an unwritten dictum that teams would not report this infraction to the league because of its common occurrence. As for the actual incident, Lambeau used three Notre Dame players in a late-season game. It is widely believed that Halas detected the ringers, alerted the *Chicago Tribune* newspapermen, who then reported the violation. Suspicion of Halas was fueled when it was determined that one of the players, Heartley "Hunk" Anderson, a former Notre Dame teammate of Lambeau's, was a player Halas badly wanted in a Bears uniform. If the Packers remained in the league, Anderson was almost certain to come to terms with the Wisconsin franchise. They didn't. On January 22, 1922, the Green Bay franchise was revoked.

The enterprising Lambeau immediately tendered an application for a franchise in his own name. Then-president Joe Carr told him he would have to wait 60 days for an answer. In reality it took Carr five months to act favorably on Lambeau's request, and by that time Halas had Anderson under contract in Chicago.

With that, the rivalry was inflamed. Both coaches prepared with maniacal zeal for their regular gridiron wars. Given their lengthy tenures, Halas and Lambeau dueled each other more than any other coaching pair. Lambeau never relented on the grudge, refusing ever to shake hands with Halas before or after a game. "Shake hands?" Lambeau

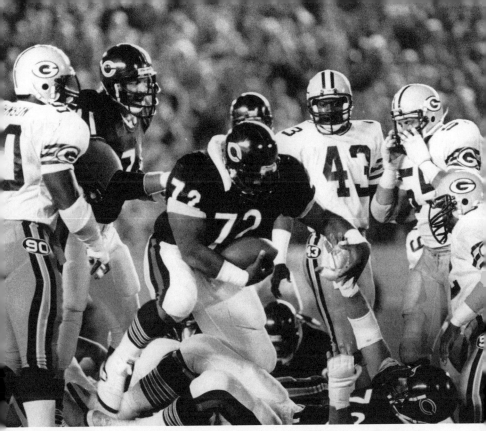

William Perry celebrated a one-yard touchdown run against the Packers in the Bears Monday Night *victory over the Packers in 1985. The Bears dominated the series against the Packers in the 1930s and 1940s and again in the 1980s.*

asked incredulously, "That would have been a lie. If I lost, I wanted to punch Halas in the nose. If he lost, Halas wanted to punch me."

The rivalry developed into the NFL equivalent of the Michigan–Ohio State annual confrontation, in part because each franchise was highly successful during the early NFL years, often standing in one another's way in the quest for championships. Over the years, play has been rougher than normal in these battles, even if no title was on the line. The gridiron wars generated missing teeth, broken bones, smashed mouths, wrenched knees, concussions, and other assorted evidence of brutally violent play. Nothing seemed dirty in this rivalry. It was what you could get by doing without being apprehended by a flag-throwing official. The cause was victory, and whatever you had to do to attain that was deemed acceptable by those on your side of the struggle.

By 1939 the rivalry had reached unparalleled levels of intensity. With the Bears and Packers certain to fight it out for the Western Division

All-Time Bears

Offensive Linemen (listed alphabetically)

George Connor—Hall of Fame Bear, was All-Pro at three positions—offensive and defensive tackle and linebacker. Member of All-Pro squad of the 1940s selected by Hall of Fame Selection Committee.

Jimbo Covert—All-Pro bulwark on the offensive line during Ditka's reign and hole-opener for Walter Payton.

Danny Fortmann—All-Pro six straight times (1938–1943) for his both-ways play at guard. Member of the Hall of Fame and All-Pro squad of the 1930s.

Ed Healey—Both-ways star, called "the most versatile tackle ever" by Halas. Member of the Hall of Fame and All-Pro squad of the 1920s.

Jay Hilgenberg—Center on the powerful Bears teams of the 1980s and perennial Pro Bowl invitee along with Covert.

Stan Jones—All-NFL four times at guard, this 1950s and 1960s star went into the Hall of Fame in 1991. Played both ways in 1962.

Olin Kreutz—Consistent Pro Bowl mainstay of Bears' line in the new millennium at center for ground-oriented team.

George Musso—Played guard and tackle, making All-Pro at both positions. Played on four NFL champion teams and is in the Hall of Fame.

George Trafton—Charter member of the Bears and among the roughest of all time, the center pioneered the one-handed snap to the tailback. In the Hall of Fame and All-Pro squad of the 1920s.

Bulldog Turner—Six-time All-Pro and on the All-Pro squad of the 1940s, Turner anchored the line at center in a Hall of Fame career.

title, Halas accused the Packers of spying on his practices in Green Bay prior to their early season, September 24 get-together. Halas reported that people with binoculars filled open windows of the houses near his team's practices. Halas even interrogated residents on the matter, who claimed they were bird-watching.

That the Bears fell 21–16 in a bitter, intense battle did nothing for Halas's digestion. The game itself reached new levels of competitive rage. Players were tossed for fighting, others left with injuries, and both teams engaged in disputes with officials. After the game, Halas charged the Packers with using illegal pass plays. Lambeau had had enough of Halas's charges. "The Bears are the last team in the world to talk about unfair tactics," Lambeau told the press, assiduously avoiding any denial of the charges. "We have tolerated the Bears' rough, dirty play long enough, and now I'm going to demand Halas either apologizes for what he said or try to prove them."

Lambeau didn't wait for an apology that he knew Halas would offer only over the Chicago coach's dead body. When the teams reengaged in the Windy City, fights broke out not only on the field, but among the 40,000 fans jammed into Wrigley Field to watch the 30–27 Bears triumph. One hyped-up Chicago partisan picked a fight with former Packers end Lavvie Dilweg. It took almost no time for the Bears fan to realize the tussle "was an error of ways, the lesson of which was learned painfully," Green Bay newspaperman Dick Flatley reported cleverly.

Wrigley Field offered the Bears a huge home-field advantage. Because it was a baseball stadium, accommodating football required some curious layouts in an effort to cram in the field. As it turned out, the north (left-field) wall was about a yard beyond the end zone, while the south end zone was abbreviated by the presence of the first-base dugout. As for the fans, those in the end zones were within a few feet of the action, while those in the upper decks were almost literally on top of it. Tarpaulins adorned the sidelines, making passing difficult for players not wanting to

TRIVIA

What did the Packers have delivered to the Bears' locker room in Green Bay before a 1984 game?

Answers to the trivia questions are on pages 182–183.

encounter them on a down-and-out. Players battled it out on the skin of the Cubs' infield and crashed occasionally into the ivy-covered brick wall in left field.

While some players were intimidated, others loved it. Packers great Tony Canadeo was among the latter. "There was such a tradition in the ballpark," he said. "If you had a relative there, you knew it. In the end zone, you'd find all your former high school pals out there, saying, 'We're going to kill you today, Tony,' but there was a closeness out there. And traditionwise, I just enjoyed it."

Long after Halas and Lambeau had departed the scene, the rivalry continued to burn brightly. Lombardi and Halas were friendly rivals, but they were indeed rivals with neither denying the emotional importance of the Bears-Packers rivalry. Not surprisingly, Vince Lombardi's first win came against the Bears by a 9–6 score before 32,150 fans in Green Bay's City Stadium on September 27, 1959. Lombardi would tell his players he was "getting that Bear itch" on Bear week and brag that he could whip the old man's butt. Conversely, it was Halas's Bears who denied Lombardi in his first attempt to win three consecutive NFL titles, not only sweeping the Packers but taking the NFL crown themselves in the process. But success against Lombardi was rare for Halas, who won only five of 18 games against Lombardi.

Later Coach Mike Ditka, the former Bear who had played in many a Bears-Packers tilt during Lombardi's tenure, said, "They don't like us, and we don't like them. That's the way football is supposed to be played. I didn't know it was supposed to be buddy-buddy. They don't pick any of ours up off the ground, and ours don't pick any of theirs up. We went through a time in pro football where there was so much pattin' guys on the butt and pickin' them up, you wonder what was going on."

No mercy was shown in this rivalry. The Bears' Richard Dent and Dan Hampton once savaged Packers quarterback Lynn Dickey 30 yards away from an interception he had thrown, knocking him out of the game. In another confrontation the Bears piled on, using William "the

Refrigerator" Perry in the backfield to smash over for a short-yardage score in a 23–7 Bears triumph. While Green Bay complained about the tactic, Coach Mike Ditka made clear that he couldn't have cared less about how the Packers felt.

The Packers delivered their own mayhem. Mark Lee, a Green Bay cornerback, was once ejected after running Walter Payton out of bounds and over the Bears' bench. Later photos showed Payton pulled Lee over the bench. In another instance, a Packers safety hammered a Bears fullback while he was watching a play. And in still another, a Packer completed a sack of Jim McMahon by dropping the quarterback head-first to the ground after carrying him in his arms for several yards.

Always in the same division of the same league, each year Bears-Packers week is always special to fans of both teams. Grudges are renewed, history is reviewed, and surliness is the mood, as a new set of Green Bay Packers and Chicago Bears players continue the nasty tradition.

Starting with a Bang

The near miss in '39 did nothing to dull Halas's enthusiasm about the coming season. Falling short to the Packers never did anything but spur him on to greater achievements, and 1940 was no different. Now 45, Halas was never more ready to dominate. He had the energy to push for the top, backed by the experience of 20 years in the game to guide his decision-making.

On the personnel front, Halas got halfback George McAfee, who had been drafted by the Eagles. In addition, he drafted center Bulldog Turner from Hardin-Simmons and halfback Ray "Scooter" McLean from St. Anselm in New Hampshire, among others. Halas made one other huge move. He installed second-year-man Sid Luckman at quarterback.

McAfee vindicated Halas's efforts to get him the first time he touched the ball on a kickoff, racing 93 yards for a score against the Green Bay Packers. Not only did the Bears romp to a 41–10 win, but they did it in Wisconsin. A bitter loss to the South Side Cardinals—a team that would win only one additional game during the '40 campaign—hardened Chicago's will, as the Bears peeled off five straight wins, running their record to 6–1. Their defeat of Green Bay 14–7 in Chicago for their sixth win put them two games ahead of the Pack in the West.

The Packers picked up a game on the Bears by splitting the next two, as Chicago stumbled against Detroit and Washington. The loss to Washington was especially rankling to Halas and his charges, who were convinced a game-changing pass-interference call should have been made against the opponents, but they were rebuffed in a 7–3 loss in the East.

The team rebounded, however, closing the campaign with a pair of wins—including a 31–23 payback to the Cardinals in the season finale—and the division was theirs with an 8–3 log. They would have their chance at avenging their grinding loss at Washington in the NFL title game, once again in the nation's capital. Washington's owner, George Preston Marshall, was unimpressed by the Bears heading into the game, saying, "The Bears are front-runners, quitters. They're not a second-half team, just a bunch of crybabies. They fold up when the going gets tough." But this was a different Bears team. George McAfee remembered, "It was real quiet on the train going down to Washington. ... We were all very intense. ..." Halas gave a rousing pregame speech, telling his team he knew they were the best football team ever assembled, and the Bears went out and won in astonishing fashion, beating the Redskins 73–0, the largest margin of victory in any NFL game, regular or postseason.

Reactions were many, but two media wags provide a good example. Bob Considine, in his syndicated newspaper column "On the Line," wrote: "The Chicago Bears massacred the Washington Redskins 73–0 yesterday. ... The unluckiest guy in the crowd was the five-buck better who took the Redskins and 70 points." Bill Stern, a famous radio broadcaster, said, "It got so bad that, toward the end, the Bears had to give up place-kicking the extra point and try passes because all the footballs booted into the stands were being kept by the spectators as souvenirs. And they were down to their last football."

The team had started off the decade with a bang. Halas and others had taken to the air in '40. Luckman threw 105 passes, completing 48 for 941 yards, placing him fourth in the league. Davey O'Brien of the Eagles, however, attempted an

George McAfee in 1949.

DID YOU KNOW . . . That 43,425 fans showed up for the playoff game in 1941 at Wrigley Field, while about 30,000 fewer (13,341) were at the NFL championship game a week later, an indication of how intense the Bears-Packers rivalry was?

incredible 277 passes—60 in a single game—hitting on 124 of them for 1,290 yards. (End Don Looney caught 58 of those tosses for 707 yards, easily outdistancing the great Don Hutson of Green Bay for the pass-receiving title.) Amazingly, however, the savvy O'Brien was outgained by Washington's Baugh, who picked up 1,367 yards in the air on exactly 100 fewer attempts than O'Brien.

With the 1941 season on the horizon, the league decided to institute playoffs in the instances of ties in divisional races, and in the case of a tied playoff game, a sudden-death overtime resolution. Meanwhile, with the Bears back on top of the NFL, the ever-competitive Halas geared up for a repeat in 1941. The campaign once again shaped up as a battle with the Packers for Western Division supremacy. Green Bay bolstered its team with the addition of Tony Canadeo, a young back from Gonzaga destined for Hall of Fame renown. The Bears, however, countered by drafting two players out of Clark Shaughnessy's 1940 Rose Bowl Stanford team, Norm Standlee and Hugh Gallarneau. Halas decided to alternate powerful Bill Osmanski with ace back George McAfee, and they along with Standlee anchored a backfield that would rush for more than 1,500 yards.

The season opened against the archrival Packers on the road. A win over the Pack could be huge for the Bears, if they wanted to make their run for a second consecutive divisional crown less daunting. Not only did the team come away with a 25–17 triumph, Chicago went on to sweep the next four, putting them one up on the Packers after five games. Then came a killer 16–14 loss to Green Bay in Chicago, and the teams were knotted at 5–1 with five left.

Five weeks later the two were still tied, each closing the campaign 10–1, putting the new playoff scenario into reality in its first year. At Wrigley Field, the venue in which they had lost to the

TRIVIA

Who had been the Bears' regular at quarterback in the years before Luckman took over?

Answers to the trivia questions are on pages 182–183.

Packers a little more than a month previous, rookie Gallarneau returned a punt 81 yards for a score in the first quarter, and the Bears were on their way to a 33–14 payback win.

TRIVIA

What news of a national tragedy occurred while teams were playing the final game of the 1941 regular season?

Answers to the trivia questions are on pages 182–183.

This time the Giants were the championship foe. It would be a classic battle between a team that relied on defense—the Giants allowing just 10.4 points per game versus an offensive juggernaut—the Bears who averaged 36 points per contest.

The offense won, 37–9. After trailing 6–3 in the first quarter, it was all Bears as Stanford rookie Standlee scored twice in the game.

The Bears were champions again, and in an even more dominant fashion than the previous year when one considers that the club's '41 record was 12–1 as opposed to 9–3 in 1940. Particularly potent was the team's offense. The championship team in '40 scored 238 regular-season points. The '41 contingent added a whopping 158 to that total—a more than 14-points-per-game increase. As overpowering as was the team's ground game, of special note is the play of third-year quarterback Sid Luckman. Not only did he complete more than 50 percent of his passes (68 of 119), but he also accomplished the rare feat of throwing for more TDs than interceptions (9–6).

With the season hardly over, Halas set his sights on reaching a new height—winning a record three consecutive NFL championships, an accomplishment he had been denied in 1934 when a loss to the New York Giants spoiled an undefeated campaign.

Blowout

No reasonable football fan could have imagined that the Bears would pummel Washington in the NFL title game in 1940. First, the game would be played in Washington, where the locals had beaten the Bruins 7–3 only a month before. Moreover, if you compared the two teams going into the contest, a slight edge went to the home team. Washington, for example, had scored 245 points in its 11 games, yielding 142, for a net points difference of +103. The Bears had run up 238 and permitted 152, for a +86 margin. That alone might have made Washington a one-and-a-half point favorite. Finally, the divisions were equal, with the East and West splitting interdivisional contests.

The NFL took another step in the direction of becoming truly big-league when it sold the radio rights to the game to the Mutual Broadcasting System. The great Red Barber called the action over 120 stations. It was the first-ever championship game carried on network radio. It must certainly have been profitable for Mutual, as the conglomerate paid only $2,500 for the rights.

Halas rolled up his sleeves in preparation for this December 8 show-down. He summoned Clark Shaughnessy, who had moved on to Palo Alto, California, to coach Stanford, for help in readying the team. Shaughnessy was an expert in employing the T formation in an era in which so many college and pro teams were in a direct snap, single-type offense. In addition, Halas watched the film of the grinding 7–3 loss with intensity and noted that the opposition had used a very predictable defense. The 5-3 formation never wavered, and the linebackers moved toward the side of the man in motion. Immediately, counterplays were inserted in the offense to keep the ballcarriers away from the linebacking corps. Shaughnessy was particularly helpful. He drafted new

The Bears swarm the Redskins' Jimmy Johnston (No. 21) in action from the 1940 championship game, a 73–0 drubbing by Chicago. Sid Luckman is making the tackle while Joe Stydahar (No. 13), Bill Osmanski (No. 9), John Siegal (No. 6), Dan Fortmann (No. 21), and George McAfee (No. 5) are there to make sure Johnston is corralled.

All-Time Bears

Quarterbacks (listed alphabetically)

Ed Brown—Pro Bowl pick in 1955 and '56, was the team's main QB for six straight years, and ranks sixth all time in Bears passing yards.

Rudy Bukich—Threw 621 times for nearly 4,500 yards and 30 TDs in '65 and '66.

Jack Concannon—Played five years in Chicago and in 1970 completed 194 passes for 2,130 yards and 16 scores.

Jim Harbaugh—Completed more passes (1,023) than any other Bears QB during a seven-year tenure.

Erik Kramer—Posted an 80.7 passing rating, best all time; threw for 29 TDs and more than 3,800 yards in 1995.

Sid Luckman—Hall of Fame Bears quarterback and first T formation signal-caller; was All-Pro five times and a member of four NFL championship teams.

Johnny Lujack—Played only four years for Chicago, but was a Pro Bowl pick in 1950 and '51 and threw 23 TD strikes in 1949.

Bernie Masterson—Pre-Luckman QB, played from 1934 to 1940 and was member of three divisional championship teams, ranking fifth in completions in 1938.

Jim McMahon—Seven years a Bear, was QB of 1985 Super Bowl champions and a Pro Bowl selection that year.

Bill Wade—The man under center for the '63 champions, his lone Pro Bowl season, ranks second all time to Luckman (137) in TD passes with 68.

terminology for the Bears' offensive plays and tightened up the blocking schemes.

Sid Luckman recalled that Halas "had given me some plays to run if the Redskins were using the same defense that had worked against us before. It had worked well then, and Halas wasn't going to let it happen again. If I saw a similar defensive lineup, we could compensate. McAfee in motion one way, Ray Nolting in motion the other, whatever, to beat the defense. We knew if they used the same defense, we had them. We'd planned against it the entire week before the game. And they used the same defense."

The defensive game plan was simple: keep the ball away from Baugh by eating the clock with a ball-control offense. With that, the game was on before 36,034 Washington partisans.

There was instant evidence that the theories of Halas and Shaughnessy were sound. On the second play of the contest fullback Bill Osmanski took off around left end and ran for a 68-yard touchdown. The only problem with the instant TD was that the ball went into the eager hands of Sammy Baugh. When Washington did not score on its possession, however, the Bears went on a mind-boggling 17-play drive, covering 79 yards before Luckman snuck in from a foot out for the second score.

The next time the Bears had the ball they didn't take as long to strike pay dirt. On the first play, fullback Joe Maniaci went around the end on a 42-yard touchdown jaunt. With still more than two minutes remaining in the first quarter the Bears were up 21–0; this against a team that had held them to but three points a month earlier. First-half scoring ended when Luckman hit end Ken Kavanaugh for a 30-yard TD strike in the second quarter, putting the Bears ahead by a 28–0 count at the half.

Luckman took the second half off, turning the signal-calling chores over to Bernie Masterson, Bob Snyder, and Saul Sherman. The triumvirate took the Bears into the end zone three more times, while the defense returned three errant Washington aerials for touchdowns. By game's end the Washington faithful were less faithful, as frustrated fans began hooting sarcastically anytime the locals executed something effectively.

The final score was 73–0.

It was the biggest blowout in NFL championship history, a record that is unlikely ever to be broken. The Bears rushed for 382 yards, needing to attempt only 10 passes. Although first downs were even, the Bears put up 501 yards of offense while Washington only had 245. Ten different Bears scored touchdowns, including two by the fairly obscure Harry Clark. As potent as the Halas-Shaughnessy-fueled offense was, however, the defense was equally staunch, holding their opponents to just 22 yards rushing and intercepting eight enemy aerials.

Six future Hall of Famers took the field for the Bears that day: Stydahar, Fortmann, Turner, Musso, Luckman, and McAfee. Other than Lee Artoe, Halas had an interior line consisting entirely of Hall of Famers. The 73 points the Bears scored in the championship game were 31 percent of the total (238) they scored in the 11 regular-season games.

Chicago personality and legend Irv Kupcinet was also a professional football referee, and he worked the game. He remembered it vividly:

> I was the head linesman that day and I, like everybody else, thought the game was a toss-up. Both teams were superb, and they had played a close game earlier in the season, which the Redskins won by only a couple of points. ... In the fourth quarter...the Bears were winning 60–0. I heard the stadium announcer on the public-address system there at Griffith Stadium say, "Your attention is directed to a very important announcement regarding the sale of seats for the 1941 Redskin season." That's all I could hear because it was greeted by thunderous boos. It was the only thing Washington fans had to make noise about all day.

G. I. Joe

With the war on, by 1942 the mythical G. I. Joe was on his way to becoming the symbol of male America. And the war truly did change the face of the NFL. Scores of players and coaches donned army fatigues, joining the war effort. As a result, rosters were dotted by "4-F" players—men who had failed their service physicals—and older than normal players. In short, the league was heavily populated with "replacement" players, making it difficult for coaches to prepare for games and for franchises to know what to expect on the field. It became a year in which teams that simply had the fewest players defecting to the military would be favorites on the field. Even worse, players would enter the service during the season, forcing coaches to adjust on the fly.

In Chicago Halas was scratching his head. The Bears lost standout performers George McAfee and Norm Standlee, and Halas had to resort to his fourth-string fullback. The team was led in rushing by previously uncelebrated Gary Familglietti with 503 yards. Late in the season he would watch future Hall of Fame stalwart Joe Stydahar become G. I. Joe Stydahar.

Halas, however, was not to be denied as he drove his depleted team through the schedule. A lopsided 44–28 opening-game win at Green Bay was followed by a 21–7 conquest of the Cleveland Rams, and that was followed with a blowout win over the crosstown Cardinals, 41–14. A 38–7 pummeling of Green Bay gave the Bears an 8–0 mark, all but sewing up the Western championship. From there the squad ripped through its final three opponents by a combined 110–7, and an undefeated 11–0 season was theirs. By season's end, however, Uncle Sam had another contributor to the war effort, none other than George Stanley Halas. On December 13 Halas joined the United States Navy, leaving the team in the hands of co-coaches Heartley "Hunk" Anderson—he of the Packers dispute two decades before—and Luke Johnsos for the championship game to be played that day. The Bears' foe was Washington, the team the Bruins had humiliated by 73 points just two years back.

Washington still had Baugh at the throttle, and Slingin' Sam had thrown for 1,524 yards, second only to Cecil Isbell of Green Bay. In addition, Baugh had struck pay dirt 16 times against 11 interceptions, again second only to Isbell (24 and 14). Although the Bears were undefeated, Baugh and his mates had gone 10–1 for the campaign. Nonetheless, they hardly appeared worthy opponents for Chicago, what with the Bears scoring 376 points against just 84 for the opposition, an incredible +292 in net points. Washington had scored just 227 and permitted 102.

Sammy Baugh intercepts Sid Luckman's pass in the 1942 championship game, won by Baugh's Redskins. Bears tackle Lee Artoe looks on hopelessly.

DID YOU KNOW ...

That Sid Luckman averaged less than 10 passing attempts per game during the 1942 regular season, less than half the number of passes the team attempted in the championship game?

The oddsmakers had the Bears installed as 22-point favorites, but apparently the Washington defense was not paying attention. Chicago, averaging nearly 35 points per game, was held scoreless in the first quarter. Twice they penetrated the Washington 30 but came up empty. The Bears defense, however, returned the favor. In the second quarter the visiting Bears struck first as Chicago's Lee Artoe returned a fumble 50 yards to put his squad up 6–0. Baugh came back with a 38-yard TD strike and with the PAT the halftime score stood at 7–6. When Andy Farkas went over from one yard out in the third quarter, the locals led 14–6.

In the fourth quarter Chicago went on a march that took them 79 yards to the Washington 1. From there Hugh Gallarneau smashed over the touchdown, only to have it nullified by a backfield-in-motion penalty. When the hometowners held on downs, the game and the championship were theirs. Washington simply shut down the Chicago ground game, holding the squad to just 69 yards. With the Bears forced to throw an uncharacteristic 20 times, the defense was alert to the air game, picking off three Chicago passes.

In 1943 the war took its toll on the league in the form of reducing its membership. With owner Dan Reeves in the military, the Cleveland Rams received league permission to take a year's sabbatical from football. Moreover, the Philadelphia and Pittsburgh franchises merged to become the Steagles. This left but eight teams, with the Western Division comprised of the two Chicago franchises, the Packers, and the Detroit Lions. Despite the shrinking number of teams, players were at a premium, because now even fathers were being drafted. The league expanded the roster limit upward to 28 to accommodate new and sudden losses to war call-ups. The league instituted another, far more important rule change for the 1943 season. It legalized free substitution, which became known as platoonery, making it no longer necessary for players to play both ways in an encounter. Many in the league opposed this new rule on the grounds that "true men" should play on both sides of the ball. Perhaps that's why few teams or coaches took advantage of the rule when it was instituted.

On the Chicago front, a familiar face returned to the roster as a tackle in 1943, to bolster the club against the talent depletion of World War II. That face belonged to 34-year-old Bronislaw Nagurski. With Halas still in the navy, co-coaches Anderson and Johnsos were at the controls. Chicago was a certain contender in the West, but Green Bay would not go away, something made abundantly evident in the opener when the Packers battled the Chicagoans to a 21–21 tie on Wisconsin turf. After five straight wins, the team awaited the Packers in Chicago. With Green Bay already a game back, a win over the hated Wisconsinites could well be the knockout blow the Bruins wanted to deliver. A 21–7 victory put the Bears up by two games, and they were never headed as they won the West with an 8–1–1 record. The team scored over 30 points per game, but the big story was the sudden emergence of Luckman, who threw for 2,194 yards and 28 touchdowns against 12 interceptions. He also became the first quarterback to throw for 400 yards in a game, passing for 433 against New York, including seven touchdowns. Harry Clark, pushed into a more prominent role in the backfield, finished third in rushing with 556 yards on just 120 carries.

With Washington tied with the New York Giants in the East, the Bears had to wait for the playoff, won by Washington by a lopsided 28–0 count. So it was not only a Chicago-Washington rematch, but also the third time the teams had played for all the chips in the last four years. If there had been any question about Luckman's being a genuine superstar, it was settled in this game, as the savvy quarterback outdueled the great Baugh, hitting on 15 of 26 passes for five TDs with nary an interception. In addition, Luckman ran for 64 yards on eight carries.

After a scoreless first quarter, Washington struck for seven to go on the board first, but a three-yard touchdown rumble by Nagurski, now at fullback, and a scoring strike from Luckman to Harry Clark put the Bears

DID YOU KNOW . . . That each of the 1943 Bears earned a $1,146 share as a winner of the NFL title game?

That in 1943 some players worked in defense plants by day, practicing with their teams at night?

up 14–7 at the half. Chicago put up 13 more in the third against seven for Washington, and by game's end the Bears ruled the pro football world by a 41–21 score, much to the approval of 34,320 patrons in Wrigley Field.

With three titles in four years, really only a championship game short of four straight, the Bears were not just the Monsters of the Midway, they were the dreaded Goliaths of the NFL. And they had won this last one in the absence of Halas, who had entrusted his squad to a pair of former Bears who knew what he wanted and delivered splendidly.

Under ordinary conditions the Bears looked poised to continue atop the NFL, but these were not ordinary conditions. At any point the war could remove another key player from any team, so winning this one was especially sweet in the face of an uncertain future for not only the Bears, but the entire NFL.

The War Rages On

The 1944 season approached in a troubled atmosphere. The war was raging on and wreaking havoc with the NFL. The Pennsylvania merger of Pittsburgh and Philadelphia was halted, with Pittsburgh dropping out, leaving the Philadelphia Eagles to continue as a stand-alone operation. Pittsburgh, however, entered another gridiron marriage, this time with the Chicago Cardinals, forming another geographical hybrid called Card-Pitt. Cleveland resumed operations, while the Brooklyn Dodgers decided to call themselves the Tigers. With the league needing 10 teams, a franchise was granted to Ted Collins, who operated his team out of Boston as the Yanks.

It was a crazy year. Sammy Baugh spent part of the season in Rotan, Texas, running his ranch, splitting time with Frank Filchock at quarterback. Moreover, Clark Shaughnessy, then coaching at Maryland, spent time working his T formation wonders for Washington. While some players returned, others left.

One of them was Sid Luckman, called into the merchant marines, and relegating him to weekend availability only. With 35-year-old Gene Ronzani as his backup, the Bears were vulnerable under center. Nonetheless, there was a title to defend and a championship to be pursued, and Chicago began the effort in Green Bay, as was its custom. The Packers, however, sent them home 0–1, beating them soundly, 42–28.

A 19–7 loss at Cleveland followed, and suddenly it was to be all uphill for the '44 squad. A win over hapless Card-Pitt (it would finish 0–10) was followed by a tie with the Lions, and then a win over Cleveland in Chicago. When the Bears smacked Green Bay 21–0 the following week, the team was 3–2–1, but still well in arrears of the 6–1 Pack. Chicago won

The war took many Bears veterans but they still managed to field a competitive team, shown here in 1942. The line from left: George Wilson, right end; Joe Stydahar, right tackle; Ray Bray, right guard; Clyde Turner, center; Dan Fortmann, left guard; Ed Kolman, left tackle; and Bob Nowaskey, left end. Backfield, from left: Hugh Gallarneau, right halfback; Gary Famiglietti, fullback; Sid Luckman, quarterback; and Ray Nolting, left halfback.

three of its final four to finish a respectable 6–3–1, but Green Bay was 8–2 and the division champion. Luckman played enough to complete 71 of 143 passes for 1,018 yards, 11 TDs, and a like number of interceptions. First-year man Bob Margarita from Brown University led the team with 463 rushing yards, good enough for fourth in the league.

Despite the shifting personnel, the Bears scored 258 points, second only to Philadelphia. The defense struggled, however, giving up 172 points, sixth in the 10-team loop. The championship run was over.

The German troops surrendered to the Allied forces in May of the following year, an answer to millions of prayers. The NFL scrambled to accommodate the effects of the anticipated end to the war, placing the roster limit back at its prewar limit of 33. Despite the German surrender, the war dragged on long enough to keep huge numbers of players out for most or all of the '45 campaign. With Halas, Ken Kavanaugh, Joe Stydahar, George McAfee, and Hugh Gallarneau still absent, the Bears fell in each of their first five games.

Joy returned briefly when they defeated the eventual 6–4 Packers 28–24 in Chicago. Halas and many of his key players returned late in the season, but it was too late to avoid a sorry 3–7 campaign. On the plus side, the team won its final two games, inspiring hope for the year to come.

The 1946 season dawned with a sense of newness in the nation. The dreaded, deadly war was over, Nazism had been vanquished, and "Johnny was marching home again, hurrah, hurrah!" The NFL had survived and was taking steps to reinvent itself, and looking different in a number of ways. Geographically, the Cleveland Rams, after a good bit of haggling and initially being turned down, were permitted to move to Los Angeles, making the National Football League truly national.

There was more. Another rival league sprung up, this one called the All-America Football Conference, founded by newspaperman Arch Ward of the *Chicago Tribune,* with teams in Brooklyn, Buffalo, Chicago (nicknamed the Rockets), Cleveland, Los Angeles, Miami, New York, and San Francisco. This league appeared more formidable, if only because it had franchises in the largest American cities and was competing directly against NFL franchises in three of them. The presence of the new league troubled the NFL owners, who were concerned about losing fans and players to the rival entity, and perhaps worse, having to enter a bidding war with the other league's owners to sign and keep prized talent, all of which would drive up salaries and other costs.

The owners decided to hire a new commissioner to replace Elmer Layden, who had served for five years. They settled on Bert Bell, the co-owner of the Pittsburgh Steelers. He was tendered a three-year contract

DID YOU KNOW . . . That in 1945 the hash marks were pushed five yards further in from the sidelines—from 15 to 20 yards in?

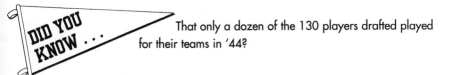

with the immediate challenge of fending off the intrusion of the rival league. Finally, opposition to free substitution remained fierce, and the owners settled on a compromise, allowing the insertion of a maximum of three players at one time.

In Chicago, optimism ruled as the team now had such key performers as McAfee, Osmanski, Gallarneau, Luckman, Turner, and Wilson back to open the season under the now 51-year-old George Halas. Getting everyone back together and in shape, however, did not go seamlessly. As George McAfee recalls, he was supposed to meet Halas in a San Francisco hotel to discuss the particulars of his rejoining the team, but when he got to the hotel at 7:00 PM the staff told him Halas had checked out. "At about midnight," McAfee said, "I thought, 'What the heck,' and I tried him again and got him. He hadn't checked out. He said he was leaving by plane in the morning for Chicago. He tried to get me on the same plane but couldn't." Instead, McAfee took a flight about an hour later, and when Halas heard about this he told McAfee to join him in Washington for that Sunday's game. "I was in lousy shape," McAfee continued, "so I started exercising there in the hotel room, anything to try and get myself into a little better shape. I got to Chicago, met up with Halas, and the same day we were on the train to Washington. I was in Honolulu on Tuesday, San Francisco on Wednesday, Chicago on Friday, and in Washington playing on Sunday, a game we lost, by the way, 28–21. It certainly was a lot different in those days in the NFL."

So even though former stars were finally returning, the task ahead for the Bears would be daunting, and not only because of rusty and out-of-shape players. The Cleveland–turned–Los Angeles Rams squad that had won the '45 title was in the Bears' five-team Western Division. So were the perennially tough Packers, along with the Detroit Lions and Chicago Cardinals.

The Jewish Prince

He wasn't tall for a quarterback, only 5'11". He was stocky, weighing 190 pounds. He was not terribly gifted physically, as a runner or passer. But he was simply a great quarterback and an out-and-out winner. His name was Sidney Luckman.

Brooklyn-born on November 21, 1916, Luckman excelled when attending Erasmus Hall high school as a prep athlete and elected to go to New York's Columbia University. There he really stood out on an otherwise mediocre team. His coach, the venerable Lou Little said, "We would have had a very ordinary team, or less than that without him." Luckman, however, made the team formidable. In 1937 he returned a kickoff 82 yards and hit on 18 of 34 passes for 202 yards against powerful Army, only to lose 21–18. Despite the humble nature of his 2–5–2 team, Luckman was named to the All-East first team by the Associated Press and to its All-America third team. In '38 he was even better, being named to a variety of All-America teams despite playing for a 3–6 team. The year's highlight was typical of Luckman's big-game heroics, this time defeating Army 20–18 with a game-winning touchdown pass.

If he learned nothing else about football at Columbia, Luckman learned to be tough as he was the target of almost every one of his opponents. "I worked behind Sid in six of his college games," recalled official Red Friesell. "In each of those games he threw at least 30 passes, and on every single one of them he was knocked nearly out of his britches by some fast-charging opponent." Despite being roughed constantly, Luckman kept his poise. "I never heard a word in protest about the beating he was taking," said Friesell.

Dexterous and agile, Luckman somehow managed to remain upright through the pounding. "The defenders were in on him most of the time,

By the NUMBERS

128—Number of games Luckman played for the Bears, who went 98–32–3 during his career.

1942—Year that Luckman led the Bears to a perfect 11–0 regular-season record.

14,686—Number of yards that Luckman passed for—a team record into the new millennium.

137—Number of TD passes Luckman threw—also a Bears record into the new millennium.

433—Number of yards Luckman once passed for in a single game.

7—Number of touchdowns Luckman once threw for in a single game.

5—Number of TD passes Luckman threw for in the 1943 NFL championship game.

3—Number of times Luckman had a passing rating above 90.0 in a prepassing era.

but he got most of his passes away as he ran from his tacklers in a hurried ballet of evasion," reported the legendary sportswriter Jimmy Cannon.

Luckman's brilliance did not float under the radar of George Halas. In fact the Bears' mentor had been following Luckman's career since his prep school days in New York and envisioned turning the spectacular halfback into a T formation quarterback for his Bears. Being an NFL player held little status in Luckman's era, and he had no intention of joining the Bears. His family discouraged him from continuing his football career and had convinced him to join the family trucking business with his brothers.

Halas was nothing if not a salesman. Intrigued by the novel Halas offense, Luckman finally signed for a then-hefty $5,000. "You and Jesus Christ are the only two people I would ever pay this to," said Halas to his Jewish prince.

"Thank you, Coach. You put me in great company," Luckman politely replied.

After a year's apprenticeship learning the complex and creative T formation offense, during which Halas used Luckman at halfback, Halas installed him under center and a Hall of Fame career was under way. Although he also played defensive back, Luckman was an All-Pro five times at the quarterback position. Luckman found the transition from playing running and defensive back to quarterback challenging, especially in a system such as Halas's. "The signal calling was diametrically opposite," Luckman said. "The spinning was very difficult because you had to be so precise and so quick. They don't do it today like we had to do it. We had counterplays and doublecounters and fakes. It was very hard for me to adjust, to get my hand under the center, and to get back and set up."

Sid Luckman attempts to run past Rams defender Tom Fears in action from this 1950s game.

His accomplishments, when viewed in the context of his time, a ground-oriented era of restricted pass blocking, are simply breathtaking. He was the league MVP in 1943, and for good reason, tossing 28 touchdown passes in just 10 games. His passing rating by today's standards was 107.5 for that year. Moreover, projected over a current 16-game season, those 28 TD strikes equate to 45, putting him in the Marino-Manning class. In fact, his 28 scores stood as a record for 16 years, before the great Johnny Unitas hit on 32 touchdown passes in the 12-game 1959 season. He led the NFL in yards per attempt five times and in total yards passing three times.

Perhaps Luckman was best known for winning. From 1940, the year Luckman took over at quarterback, through his final season in 1950, the Bears posted a 90–29–3 record, winning five division titles and four NFL crowns.

Luckman was always a favorite of Halas. The coach admired the intelligence and character of his quarterback, crediting him for being a self-made superstar. "Sid made himself a great quarterback," said an admiring Halas. "No one else did it for him. He worked hard, stayed up nights studying, and really learned the T.

"Sid wasn't built for quarterback," Halas remarked. "He was stocky, not fast, and not a great passer in the old tradition. But he was smart and he was dedicated."

Halas saw Luckman as a gridiron near-revolutionary. "In Sid we created a new type of football player, the T quarterback," reflected Halas. "Newspapers switched their attention from the star runners to the quarterbacks. It marked a new era for the game."

There were few qualities Halas cherished more than loyalty. In 1946 the Chicago Rockets of the rival All-America Football Conference dangled $25,000 under the nose of the Bears superstar Luckman to entice him to be the team's quarterback and coach. It was an eye-popping offer, not to mention an incredible opportunity.

Despite its being too good to be true by almost anyone's standards, including Luckman's, the quarterback turned it down out of loyalty to Halas, to whom he felt indebted for patiently staying with the struggling Luckman when he was laboring to master the T formation offense. "How could I have possibly taken it?" he asked rhetorically. "How could I quit a club that has done so much for me?"

After his career, Luckman served for 14 years as a part-time coach for the Bears and other teams to which Halas wanted to teach the T. He would not accept a salary out of gratitude to Halas and the Bears.

Halas wasn't the only one to realize Luckman's greatness. As the engineer of the Bears' 73–0 Washington whitewash in 1940, *The New York Times* wrote, "No field general ever called plays more artistically. He was letter-perfect." As a college senior he once adorned the cover of *Time* magazine, with the simple "Best Passer" caption. In 1965 he was inducted into the Pro Football Hall of Fame, in addition to being a member of the International Jewish Hall of Fame. In 1988 the 71-year-old Luckman received the Walter Camp Distinguished American of the Year Award. He died 10 years later.

Back on Top

If Halas knew anything, he knew the importance of getting out of the gate swiftly. The past two unhappy seasons were characterized by early season defeats, losses from which the team simply was unable to recover. That could not be permitted to happen in 1946. First came the customary opener against the hated Packers in Green Bay, a game that all too often was nearly determinative, despite its being the opener.

Determinative or not, the Bears laid the lumber to the Pack in front of a legion of unhappy Wisconsinites, 30–7. The Cardinals fell the following week, 34–17, setting up a huge confrontation with the Rams in Chicago. Despite putting up 28 points, all the Chicagoans could muster was a tie, leaving the now 2-0-1 team one full game ahead of the Californians at 1-1-1. After winning two of their next three, the 4-1-1 Bruins headed west to face off with the 3-2-1 Rams. When the Bears emerged with a 27–21 win, Halas's team never looked back.

Chicago went on to lock up the West with an 8-2-1 mark, two full games in front of defending champion Los Angeles and two and a half ahead of both the Cardinals and Packers, knotted at 6–5. The team was by no means dominating during the season, posting 289 points on offense, good enough to lead the league, but yielding 193, placing it a mediocre fifth in a 10-team NFL. Perhaps the Bears' middling statistics were due to the competitive nature of the Western Division, which sported four teams with winning records, the Bears, Rams, Packers, and Cardinals. The division was balanced by Detroit's going 1-10-0.

This time it was the New York Giants that stood in the way of the Bears' effort to reclaim their position atop the NFL. The Giants had no one ranking in the top five in rushing, passing, or receiving, but they managed to win seven games, losing three and tying one. The Bears, however, featured Hugh Gallarneau, who ranked fourth in rushing with 476 yards, and of course the great Sid Luckman, who threw for 1,826 yards and 17 touchdowns.

The New Yorkers were not as strong on offense (236 points) but a tad better on the other side of the ball (162). Despite Chicago's slight edge in positive net points (96 to 74), with the game in the Big Apple the challenge would be substantial.

The league was delighted when a throng of 58,346 showed up at the Polo Grounds for the December 15 confrontation. The Bears were growling early as they put up 14 quick first-quarter points, on a 21-yard TD strike from ace quarterback Luckman to Ken Kavanaugh, followed by a 19-yard interception return by secondary man Dante Magnani. Frank Filchock answered, however, with a 38-yard scoring toss, but that closed the scoring in the first half. Chicago's 14–7 lead melted in the third canto when Filchock delivered a five-yard scoring aerial to Steve Filipowicz, on the heels of a Bears fumble and roughing-the-quarterback infraction.

The game entered the final quarter tied at 14, and Halas most certainly was nervous. Then, however, Sid Luckman took over. He bamboozled the New York defense with a play called "97-bingo, keep it." On the opponent's 19, Luckman surveyed the New York defense and called for time. He went over to Halas and asked a one-word question, "Now?" Halas's response was the same word in the affirmative, "Now." The play to which they were referring was a special trap play, one in which Luckman faked a handoff to speedy George McAfee, concealed the ball on his hip, and took off around right end while the Giants defenders were suckered into following the Chicago line moving away from the play. Luckman did not go in unmolested, having to fight off a would-be tackler at the 10 and utilizing key blocks by Bulldog Turner and Ray Bray before hitting pay dirt for what would be the winning score in a 24–14 win. Luckman remembered the 1946 championship game as "the most vicious football game I'd ever played in my life. There was the toughest tackling, the fiercest blocking, the hardest running."

The game was closer than the final score indicated, with the two teams

TRIVIA

Despite battling it out with the competing All-America Football Conference, what news brought great happiness to the NFL owners in 1946?

Answers to the trivia questions are on pages 182–183.

Sid Luckman (left), George McAfee, and Ray McLean (right) celebrate the Bears'
24–14 victory over the New York Giants at the Polo Grounds in the 1946
championship game.

within three yards of one another in total yardage—248–245 in New
York's favor. Moreover, the Giants picked up 13 first downs, three more
than Chicago.

No matter. The Bears were back on top of the National Football League.

There were rumors of a betting scandal involving the 1946 championship game. Frank Filchock, who had come over from Washington to
help lead the Giants to the Eastern Division championship, and Merle
Hapes were pulled aside and interrogated as to their knowledge of a New
York man's attempts to fix the game. There was fire under the smoke to
the extent that Hapes was suspended from the game for not reporting
the contact. Filchock, however, was allowed to play. Filchock, by performing well, took a major step toward vindicating himself.

In 1947 the Bears were back to their old ways. They lost at Green Bay
(29–20) and then took a 31–7 walloping on the South Side of the Windy
City at the hands of the Cardinals. Halas had good reason to be concerned.

That in 1947 the owners decided that one team each year would get a special "bonus" draft choice? This was a real potential plum, as the choice preceded the rest of the draft. The Bears were the fortunate recipients of the first-ever bonus draft choice opportunity. They chose a back, Bob Fenimore from Oklahoma A&M (later Oklahoma State). Fenimore lasted one year.

That was not the only new rule, as the league continued to tinker with the game. Sudden death was made a part of the championship game rules, and a fifth official was added to each crew. In addition, teams were allotted 35 players for the first three games, 34 thereafter.

Not for long, however, as the team reeled off eight straight wins to run its record to 8–2. Now a game in front of the second-place Cardinals, the Bears readied for an invasion of Wrigley Field by the Rams.

After beating them 41–21 in Los Angeles earlier in the season, the Rams exacted some revenge, dealing the Bears a tough 17–14 loss. With the Cardinals finishing off the Eagles in Philadelphia by a lopsided 45–21, the Bears had dropped into a dead heat with the South Siders with only one game to go. And that game matched the two for the Western Division championship. Fortunately the game was to be played at Wrigley Field, but the Cardinals scored first and went on to win the intracity championship battle by a 30–21 count, a victory made especially precious given the team's longstanding tradition as an NFL bottom-feeder.

The Bears were arguably the better team, putting up 363 points and yielding 241 (a +122), while the Cardinals defense held their opponents for just 10 fewer points (231) but were no match for the Bears offense, scoring 306 points. It didn't matter. The Cardinals were heading for the title game, and when the Cardinals defeated the Philadelphia Eagles 28–21 before 30,759 on a frozen field at Comiskey (White Sox) Park in the title game, Chicago had a reason to celebrate, except that the celebration belonged to the city's South Side.

Luckman, Kavanaugh, and tackle Fred Davis made All-Pro. The Bears' quarterback, in the absence of a scintillating ground game, threw 323 times for a very substantial 2,712 yards. But as much as he lived by the aerial sword, the great Luckman died by the same weapon, throwing 31 interceptions in the process.

Closing Out the '40s

Halas knew the Cardinals were not necessarily a one-year wonder. The South Side squad had what was called a "dream backfield," consisting of Charlie Trippi, Elmer Angsman, Pat Harder, and quarterback Paul Christman. The latter was considered a topflight signal caller—having ranked fifth in passing in '47, while the other three were each All-Pro during their careers, with Trippi eventually enshrined in Canton. Clearly, the Cardinals figured to be the team for the Bears to beat as they prepared to do battle in 1948.

Another battle was also taking place, however. It was between the established NFL and the upstart All-America Football Conference. Not only did the rival league not roll over and die, but it was now fighting it out with the NFL for playing talent. The AAFC also had some savvy owners, not the least of whom was the venerable Branch Rickey, considered by many to be the smartest front-office operator of all time in America's then–No. 1 sport, baseball. Rickey, the man in charge of the Brooklyn Dodgers, was the owner of the AAFC team of the same name.

During the '48 draft, Washington had the bonus choice and chose Harry Gilmer, a tailback from Alabama. With Sammy Baugh up in years, owner George Preston Marshall looked to Gilmer to develop into Slingin' Sam's successor. With both Baugh and Gilmer in the fold, Marshall sold the rights to Charlie Conerly from Mississippi to the New York Giants. The Giants wound up dueling Rickey and the Dodgers before eventually signing Conerly, who would lead the team to championships as a quarterback. Y. A. Tittle, however, escaped the NFL Lions and signed with the Baltimore Colts of the rival league.

In Chicago, the Bears added rookies George Connor and Johnny Lujack from Notre Dame, along with Bobby Layne from Texas. Layne had been drafted by Pittsburgh but didn't want to operate out of the single wing, so Pittsburgh worked out a deal with the Bears. Layne didn't come cheaply. Halas wound up signing him for $22,500 in a battle with the AAFC. George Connor, a collegiate star at Notre Dame, also received a hefty bonus of $6,000. News of the bonus reached the Bears' locker room, and many were not too happy that a rookie was making more than the established players. Connor recalled, "When I went to my first training camp, I found out just how poorly that sat with the other players. They really gave me a hard time. We scrimmaged a lot, we had intrasquad games, and they were really after me. Most of the scars I have on my face today are from my teammates that year. But I was able to ward them off and got through the camp scrimmages with a variety of bruises, scabs, and pains."

Chicago started the season with four straight wins, none by less than 11 points. Moreover, Chicago's victims included the Packers and the

Johnny Lujack (left) won the 1947 Heisman Trophy playing for Notre Dame. Presenting the award is Wilbur Jurden, president of the Downtown Athletic Club.

DID YOU KNOW . . . That the Bears finished either first or second in the Western Conference in every year of the 1940s except 1945?

Cardinals, putting the Bears up by a game on the Cardinals coming out of the blocks. A tough 12–7 loss at Philadelphia was followed by six straight wins, giving Chicago a sparkling 10–1 record going into the final game of the season.

That was the good news. The bad news was that the Cardinals did not lose a single game other than that early season loss at home to the Bears, hence as the two teams met in Wrigley Field in the finale, each team came in with a 10–1 mark. Once again the Cardinals defeated the Bears on the final day of the season, this time by a maddening 24–21 margin. Once again the Bears held a substantial edge in net points (+224 as opposed to +169), but this time it was the Cardinals who had the high-voltage offense, outscoring the Wrigley Field North Siders by a 395–375 margin. Trippi and Angsman finished 2–3 in rushing for the Cards, while the Bears failed to place anyone among the league's elite (top five) in rushing, passing, or pass receiving. (The Cardinals' powerful offense that averaged nearly 33 points per game in the regular season failed to score a single point in the championship game with Philadelphia. With a blizzard blanketing Shibe Park, wiping out the yard lines, the Eagles took the title, 7–0. The conditions were so severe that the lights were turned on, and Commissioner Bell directed the officials not to measure using the 10-yard down markers and chain, but to determine first downs on the field.)

By 1949 the NFL was really feeling the effects of competing with the AAFC. The champion Eagles were operating in the red and had to be sold to a syndicate of buyers. The Packers, who had competed the most intensely with the rival league, were in severe financial duress. The Boston Yanks moved to New York as the Bulldogs, sharing the Polo Grounds with the Giants. Meanwhile in Chicago two bridesmaid finishes galled the always competitive Halas as he got his team ready to regain the NFL crown in 1949. Prior to the season he traded Layne to the New York Bulldogs of the Eastern Division. (The Bulldogs were the former Boston Yanks.) Luckman, now nearing the end of his career, developed a thyroid problem, sidelining the ace for much of the season and pressing Lujack into duty under center.

Once again the Bears were in the thick of the race. This time it was neither the Cardinals nor the Packers with which they contended. The Cardinals finished 6–5–1, while the Packers hit bottom at 2–10. Chicago started the season knocking off Green Bay and the Cardinals, both on the road, by 17–0 and 17–7 scores, respectively. A convincing third-week loss at home to Los Angeles, 31–16, left Chicago with a 2–1 mark, a game behind the conquering Rams. A win over the Eagles was followed by a 35–28 loss to the Giants at New York, and the Bears were 3–2 and heading to Los Angeles for a must-win return engagement with the 5–0 Rams.

When the Rams edged Chicago by a 27–24 count, the Bears were three games out with half a season remaining, and the sky looked dark. Chicago then went on a tear, winning the next five in a row, while the Rams won only one. When the Cardinals took out the Rams in the second to the last week, 31–27, the standings had the Rams at 7–2–2 and the Bears at 8–3.

1940s Bears Greats

Sid Luckman—Despite the attention-getting brilliance of Sammy Baugh, Luckman had no equal when it came to winning.

Clyde "Bulldog" Turner—Turner was by far the best lineman on the team, if not in the entire league, throughout the '40s. Willing and able to play a variety of positions, including running back, he was almost always front and center whenever there was a Bears success.

George McAfee—McAfee was the backfield equivalent of Turner, capable of performing brilliantly at any skill position.

George Musso—Great as Musso was in the '30s, his career stretched to 1944, placing him on four more division champions and three more NFL champions.

One of the highlights of the season was Johnny Lujack's game against the Chicago Cardinals in the finale. He threw for 469 yards and six touchdowns in the 52–21 romp over the Cards. Many insist, however, that Lujack was an even better defensive back, where he played regularly in the era of two-way service. Lujack's heroics weren't enough as Los Angeles routed Washington the same afternoon to claim the division title with an 8–2–2 mark to the Bears' 9–3.

TRIVIA

Bears great Bill Hewitt wore now-retired No. 56 during his sterling career. Bronko Nagurski, Bulldog Turner, George McAfee, and Sid Luckman also had their numbers retired. Do you know which numbers they wore?

Answers to the trivia questions are on pages 182–183.

Despite the bitter ending to the decade—with three straight near misses—the Bears were truly a dominant force once again in the 1940s. Chicago was 81–26–3 for the 10 years. Moreover, the run included nine winning seasons, five division championships, and four NFL titles. Though never wanting to finish second to anyone in anything at any time, Halas had come a long way from Decatur, Illinois. Through intelligence, creativity, hard work, and persistence he had an NFL franchise that was the envy of the football world.

The Speed and the Power

He hailed from Ironton, Ohio, true football country, though born across the border in Corbin, Kentucky, on March 13, 1918. His career stretched almost perfectly through the '40s, beginning at the outset of the decade for the first two years, then running from 1945 to 1950. As such it was not particularly lengthy, much of it lost to military service. When he did play, however, George McAfee left an indelible mark on opponents and in the memories of Bears fans of his time.

Much was expected of the Duke All-American; he was the team's top draft choice in '40, after Halas traded three linemen to Philadelphia to gain his draft rights. Duke coach Wallace Wade recounted McAfee's skills: "He was really a one-man offense and practically unstoppable. He was a great kicker, great runner, great passer, and one of the best receivers I've ever seen." In Chicago, however, there was concern that the rather slight—6'0", 165-pound—McAfee might simply be too small for the mayhem that was the NFL in that era. The Duke star quickly dispelled that notion, establishing himself as a breakaway threat immediately. He returned a kickoff 75 yards for a score in his very first exhibition game. In the season opener of 1940, "One Play McAfee" ran back a kickoff 93 yards and threw a TD pass to help sink the Packers, 41–10, in the Bears' championship campaign.

Used as a spot back during his first two seasons, McAfee tied Don Hutson's touchdown record in 1941, hitting pay dirt a dozen times. The 1941 season put McAfee on the pro football map. He averaged 7.3 yards per rush (474 yards), snared seven passes for 144 yards (20.6 per catch), intercepted six passes, and scored 12 touchdowns, easily sufficient to be named to every All-Pro team of that year.

When the war came there was nothing to consider for the patriotic McAfee. "I didn't want to be drafted," he explained. "I enlisted as did so many other young men. I felt like it was my duty and the thing to do."

When he returned, a knee injury hampered his effectiveness in '46. "After I hurt my knee I couldn't run like I had before, so I was happy to play mostly defense," McAfee recalled. Despite the injury he continued to rush and catch passes and managed to score eight touchdowns.

McAfee's strength was his versatility. He played both ways—could run from scrimmage, pass, and especially return kicks. On the defensive side, the fleet, athletic McAfee picked off opponent aerials. His career numbers, testimony to his multifaceted skills, were good enough to get him into the Hall of Fame, class of 1966:

- 1,685 yards rushing on 341 attempts—a 4.9 average and 22 touchdowns
- 85 pass receptions for 1,359 yards— 16.0 average and 10 touchdowns
- 1,431 yards on 112 punt returns— a record 12.8 average and two touchdowns
- 25 pass interceptions, returning them 350 yards—two touchdowns

A grateful man, McAfee enjoyed his years as a Bear and after. "Pro football was a wonderful part of my life," he recalled. "I thoroughly enjoyed my

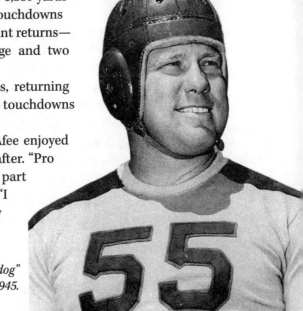

Clyde "Bulldog" Turner in 1945.

All-Time Bears

Running Backs (listed alphabetically)

Neal Anderson—Four-time Pro Bowl performer and three-time 1,000-yard rusher; was the great Payton's successor.

Rick Casares—Tough fullback of the '50s and '60s, led the NFL in rushing in 1956 with 1,126 yards in a dozen games; five times in the Pro Bowl.

Beattie Feathers—First-ever NFL 1,000-yard rusher in his rookie year (1934); averaged 5.8 yards per carry in his four-year tenure.

Willie Galimore—Averaged 4.5 yards per rush in a seven-year career that ended with a fatal car crash in 1964; Pro Bowl pick in 1958.

Thomas Jones—Averaging better than four yards per carry, has gained more than 2,200 yards in '04 and '05 on more than 550 attempts.

George McAfee—Hall of Fame speed back during the 1940s with career interrupted by military service, averaged 4.9 yards per attempt.

Bronko Nagurski—Hall of Fame powerhouse fullback who was the yardstick by which other NFL power runners were measured; averaged 4.4 yards per carry.

Bill Osmanski—Member of four NFL championship squads; led NFL in rushing in his first year (1939) as a Bear with 699 yards and 5.8 per carry.

Walter Payton—Arguably the greatest football player of all time; was the NFL all-time leading rusher when he concluded his 13-year Bears career.

Gale Sayers—Enshrined in the Hall of Fame for a career in which he played only 68 games, yet made the Pro Bowl squad four times, and led the NFL in rushing twice.

association with the Bears." Nonetheless, McAfee held the game in perspective. "But it was part of my life, just like college was a part, and I am in another part now that I'm retired. You had better believe there is life after pro football, and it is a good life. I have a lovely wife, nice children, and we are happy as larks down here in Durham [North Carolina, site of Duke University]."

Born March 10, 1919, in Plains, Texas, Clyde "Bulldog" Turner was not a breakaway threat. On the contrary, the 6'1", 237-pound Turner was a center out of Hardin-Simmons who played from 1940 to 1952 in Chicago. During Turner's college era, pro teams relied heavily on magazines and preseason All-America picks to locate college prospects. Despite playing at less than famous Hardin-Simmons, Turner was noticed when a fan alerted Bears scout Frank Korch to Turner's prowess during the young man's junior year. Korch informed Halas, who made Turner his top draft choice in 1940.

Unlike the diminutive McAfee, there was no doubt about Turner right from the outset, and Halas put the rookie in the starting lineup in 1940. Over time, Turner simply became a bulwark on the Chicago line. He was a ferocious blocker, able to play guard or tackle as well as center. As with McAfee, Turner was versatile, willing to do what was necessary to win. During war-ravaged 1944, Bulldog occasionally played in the backfield, grinding out precious yardage, including one run for 48 yards. A fearsome linebacker on defense with uncommon speed for a big man, he led the league in interceptions, with eight in 1942. Turner claimed to study all 11 assignments on each play. It proved wise when a number of his fellow Bears were ejected for unseemly contact in a 1943 game.

Turner was named to All-Pro teams seven times and proved a clutch player by intercepting five passes in championship games. A virtual iron man in a 60-minute-man era, Hall of Fame teammate George Musso said of Turner, "Who knows what kind of player he would have been if he ever got to rest during a game?" The 13-year Bears veteran died in 1998 at 79.

Appropriately, Turner and McAfee—the speed and the power of the mighty Bears of the 1940s—were both inducted into the Pro Football Hall of Fame in 1966.

A New Era

It was 1950 and more than the beginning of the second half of the 20th century in the National Football League. It was a new era, and the NFL had a very new look, given the absorption of three teams from the now-defunct All-America Football Conference. Rather than Eastern and Western Divisions, there were now American and National Conferences. The Bears were members of the seven-team National Conference, along with Los Angeles, Detroit, Green Bay, and three new teams, the New York Yanks, Baltimore Colts, and San Francisco 49ers. The Cardinals moved to the East.

The major rule change was the reinstitution of completely free substitution, opening the door to two-platoon football and other forms of specialization. Among the more intriguing games on the '50 schedule was a season-opening contest between the reigning NFL champion Philadelphia Eagles and the four-time AAFC champion Cleveland Browns. The Browns struck a mighty blow in favor of the AAFC by pounding the Eagles 35–10. Cleveland went on to beat every team on its schedule other than the New York Giants—who beat them twice—to go 10–2 and tie the Giants in the American Conference. When the Browns prevailed 8–3 in a playoff game with New York, the team from the AAFC was in the NFL championship contest.

The Bears opened the 1950 campaign on the West Coast with a 24–20 win over the Rams followed by a 32–20 conquest of the 49ers. A 31–21 loss to the weak (3–9 on the season) Packers team on the road sat in Halas's craw, but the team went on to win five of the next six, putting the Bears' record at 7–2 with just three games remaining. The Rams were next, in Wrigley Field, with what figured to be the championship on the line. Los Angeles had lost only one game since the opener to the Bears

DID YOU KNOW . . . That the streak of six straight winning seasons from 1946 to 1951 was only the third-best such streak in Bears history? The team posted nine straight winners from its inception as the Staleys in 1920 to 1928 and then ran off an incredible 15 from 1930 to 1944.

and held a half-game lead with an 8–2 mark. Realizing what was at stake, the two hammered it out in Chicago, with the Bears coming away with a 24–14 win.

Only two games were left—a visit to the South Side to play the 4–6 Cardinals and a date at home against the 6–5 Detroit Lions. Despite having put away the Cardinals by three TDs, 27–6, earlier in the year, the Bears got tangled up in a titanic struggle with the South Siders, eventually losing by a 20–10 score. A tight 6–3 win the following week gave Chicago a 9–3 mark, identical to that of the Rams, a team they had beaten twice during the campaign and now would have to play once again in a playoff in Los Angeles.

The game matched the potent Rams offense against the Chicago defense. The Rams had rung up 466 points in 12 games against just 309 for the Bears, while the Bears allowed only 207 points compared to 309 for Los Angeles. The Rams air game was just too much, with the great Tom Fears snaring three touchdown passes, and the Bears were turned into bridesmaids once again, 24–14. Fears had won the pass-receiving championship by an insane 32 receptions. Cleveland won it all, however, defeating the Rams 30–28 on a Lou Groza field goal with 28 seconds left in Los Angeles for the NFL crown.

The campaign to catch the Rams in the National Conference proved futile once again for the Bears in 1951. The season could hardly have opened more auspiciously, with Chicago taking five of its first six to post a 5–1 mark at the halfway point. Then the team hit the wall. After splitting its next two, the Bears dropped a pair (to the Browns and the Rams), giving the team a far less lustrous 6–4 record. An easy 45–21 triumph over the New York Yanks in New York pushed the club's record to 7–4, and heading into the final week of the season the Lions led the Bears and Rams by just a half game. Detroit fell at San Francisco in the season finale, 21–17, while the Rams hammered the Packers by a 42–14 count. When the Bears were once again stunned by the 2–9 Cardinals, 24–14, it

TRIVIA

Who was the Cardinals coach when the team hung those tough losses on the Bears in 1950 and 1951?

Answers to the trivia questions are on pages 182–183.

cost them a piece of the National Conference championship.

Despite finishing only one game behind the Rams, Chicago actually landed in fourth place, as the Lions and 49ers tied for second with 7–4–1 records. Finishing out of the money by a nose was maddening for the Bears and their loyal fans. The 1951 season made it five consecutive near misses. Chicago had posted a 43–17 record from 1947 to 1951, and yet failed to win a single division or conference championship.

After six straight winning seasons the string came to an end in 1952 as the Bears sunk to 5–7–0. Quarterback was a major headache for Halas as Johnny Lujack retired after the 1951 season, heading for Notre Dame to assist Irish legend Frank Leahy. As a result, the signal-calling duties were divided among three young players—Steve Romanik, Bob Williams, and George Blanda. Despite its offensive woes, Chicago's defense definitely needed work, because the team allowed more than 27 points per game, hardly the norm for a Halas-coached contingent. The future, however, did not look bleak. George Connor was developing into a major force, and 1952 was the first season for defensive back Jim Dooley, end Bill McColl, and future Hall of Fame linebacker Bill George.

Out of Wake Forest, George became one of the legends of the '50s and '60s Bears as the team's brilliant middle linebacker, calling defensive signals for eight seasons.

Success was more than a year away, however, as the Bears nearly scraped bottom in the Western Conference in 1953, a year which marked the return of the Eastern and Western labels, this time as conferences rather than divisions. More momentous was the upholding of Commissioner Bell's new league policy allowing teams to televise only their road games.

Chicago salvaged a bit of pride, if not the season, when on the 10th week of the season it defeated the powerful Rams 24–21, dealing their championship hopes a fatal blow. The team finished with a 3–8–1 mark, putting them just a game ahead of the cellar-dwelling 2–9–1 Packers, and a half game better than Baltimore.

Doug Atkins, who came over from the Browns in 1955, turned out to be a great player and a colorful character to boot, one who had his clashes with Halas.

Atkins would dial it up even higher when angry, something no opponent wished. Unafraid of the autocratic Halas, Atkins was a consistent thorn in the owner-coach's flesh, frequently getting into tiffs with his mentor. Nonetheless, Halas said there had never been a better defensive end than Doug Atkins.

Halas's grandson and future president of the Chicago Bears, Michael McCaskey, heard many stories about Atkins while growing up.

Doug's run-ins with my grandfather were legendary. One story comes to mind. Halas made a big deal about a player's weight,

Doug Atkins holds a bust of himself after being inducted into the Pro Football Hall of Fame on August 7, 1982.

and he would fine a player for every pound he was overweight. He even instituted a "fat man's table" at camp to control the diet of those guys who needed to lose weight. Doug battled the weight thing all the time. Different players had different ways of getting the weight off. ... Atkins found a unique approach one year. Wednesday ordinarily was the weigh-in day, and Doug walked up to my grandfather on one Tuesday, and he had one of these big paper cups full of Ex-Lax. He said, "Coach, is there gonna be a weigh-in tomorrow?" Halas looked at him and said, "Tomorrow's Wednesday, isn't it?" Then Doug, right in front of him, downed this enormous cup of Ex-Lax. My grandfather stared at him all the way through it; when Doug finished chewing, Halas announced, "No weigh-in tomorrow."

Atkins had an immediate and sudden impact on the Bears defense. The Tennessee All-American started his career in Cleveland, but joined the Bears after two seasons and immortalized himself in Chicago. The monstrous 6'8", 257-pound defensive end would leapfrog over offensive linemen in a maniacal quest of sacking the quarterback. He was named to eight Pro Bowl teams and was an All-Pro pick four times.

Quarterbacks were well aware of Atkins. "He is the strongest man in football and also the biggest," said Hall of Famer Fran Tarkenton. "When he rushed the passer with those oak tree arms of his way up in the air, he is 12' tall. And if he gets to you, the whole world suddenly starts spinning." Johnny Unitas, another Hall of Fame quarterback remarked of Atkins's strength, "One of his favorite tricks was to throw a blocker at the quarterback."

Jim Parker, as outstanding a lineman as has ever played the game, called Atkins the meanest player he had ever played against. "After my first meeting with him," said Parker, "I really wanted to quit pro football. Finally my coaches convinced me [that] not every pro player was like Atkins."

Changing of the Guard

In 1954 George Halas was 59 years old and not happy. The Bears, the fans, and especially the owner-coach were tired of losing. His team had lost 15 games over the past two seasons, two more than its total over the previous four.

Things had to change. The season opened badly with a convincing 48–23 spanking at the hands of Detroit. Two wins were followed by two losses, leaving the Bears at a disappointing 2–3. That was followed by a 31–27 win at San Francisco and another 28–23 win, this time over the Packers, pushing the team mark to 4–3. The Cleveland Browns then came to Chicago and taught the Bears some lessons in a 39–10 punishment.

A 4–4 record was not what Halas had in mind for '54. The coach then drove his team to four consecutive wins down the stretch, capping the furious close with a 28–24 win over Western Division champion Detroit in the final game of the season. The team's 8–4 record put them back in a familiar place, second in the conference. Detroit was 9–2–1.

In 1954 the Bears took to the air. The team had drafted Georgia standout Zeke Bratkowski, and the rookie shared quarterback duties with Blanda. The two combined for more than 3,000 passing yards, with more than 1,000 of them being hookups with prized rookie Harlon Hill out of tiny Florence State Teachers College in Alabama. The team also got a boost on the offensive line, as Stan Jones of Maryland and Larry Strickland from North Texas State started as rookies. On a less happy note, the team felt the loss of stellar tackle George Connor, who was lost for the season with an injury.

Off the field the Bears were part of a much more solid NFL. The owners, realizing the excellent work of Bert Bell guiding them through the financial wars with the AAFC, awarded the commissioner with a remarkable 12-year contract.

By 1955 the 60-year-old Halas had had enough. He announced that the '55 campaign would be his last as coach. The prospect of getting out, however, did nothing to quell his desire to win. He had to wait, though, as the Bears dropped their first three games, losing to the Packers, Colts, and 49ers.

Shades of 1954, as Chicago tore through their next six games, and after nine contests Chicago was 6–3. A devastating 53–14 upset at the hands of the struggling South Side Cardinals in Game 10, however, spoiled the season. Chicago finished 8–4–0, a frustrating half game behind the Rams at 8–3–1. It was an unsatisfying way for Halas to exit.

The team did make some strides. With rookie running backs Rick Casares and Bobby Watkins in the starting lineup and each averaging more than five yards a carry, the rushing game got a push. With Bratkowski in the service, Ed Brown, a second-year quarterback out of San Francisco, stepped in, throwing for 1,307 yards on the strength of a 51.8 percent completion rate.

Bears great George Connor retired at the end of the '55 season. He hailed from Holy Cross and Notre Dame, having begun at the former, entered the service, and then finished in South Bend. He was an All-American at both schools and he was the first-ever winner of the Outland Trophy in 1946, given to the top college lineman. Just a tremendous player, he was All-NFL at three positions—offensive tackle, defensive tackle, and linebacker.

So George Halas stepped down again as coach after the season. Since the '20s he had been coaching the Bears, with great success. What would he do now? Irv Kupcinet said years before "they tried to persuade George to run for mayor of Chicago. It was Don Maxwell of the *Tribune*. He was convinced that George, with his great following in the city, could be the savior of the Republican party. Chicago had not had a Republican mayor since Big Bill Thompson left office in 1931." Halas declined the offer, noting to Kupcinet that if he ran as a Republican, "the first thing that would happen to me is the Bears would lose all their Democratic fans. I don't want to split my following." So Halas stuck with overseeing the Bears—but from the sidelines.

The 1956 edition of the Chicago Bears belonged to John "Paddy" Driscoll. Driscoll, a former teammate and coaching aide to Halas, started out badly, losing the opener 28–21 in Baltimore. A week later, however, his Bears vanquished the Pack 37–21 in cheese country and followed that with wins in each of the next six games. A tie with the Giants in New York put Chicago at 7–1–1, a half game ahead of the Lions,

John "Paddy" Driscoll (right) became head coach of Chicago in 1956, only the fifth different head coach in Bears history to that point.

DID YOU KNOW ... That prior to 1955 players could continue to advance after being knocked to the turf until they were stopped? To curb excessively rough play a rule was put in declaring the ball dead the instant any part of the player's body, other than his hands and feet, hit the ground after being in the grasp of an opponent. The following season the rule was tightened to any time as a result of contact.

their next opponents. Clearly the game in the Motor City was critical, and the fans expected a squeaker.

It didn't squeak. Instead the Lions roared to an easy 42–10 victory to take the lead in the Western Conference. The following week the Lions beat the Steelers and the Bears trimmed the Cardinals, setting up a season-ending showdown between the Bears and Lions in Wrigley Field. This time the result was different, as Driscoll's Bruins romped to a 38–21 win to take the conference with a 9–2–1 mark, a nose ahead of Detroit at 9–3.

The Bears had their stars in '56. Rugged Rick Casares pounded out a league-leading 1,126 yards in just 234 carries, while Ed Brown hit on 57 percent of his throws, leading the league in passing, and Harlon Hill was fourth in receiving with 47 catches. Casares ran for 12 touchdowns, the same number for which Brown threw.

Also joining the Bears in the '50s was Stan Jones. Jones became one of the greatest linemen of all time. He was selected to seven straight Pro Bowls (1956–1962) and All-NFL four times. He is credited as the first to rely on weight training for football preparation. Extremely durable, he was the team's offensive captain for a number of years. Jones played guard and remembers that "guards in those days were usually around 230 pounds. I was playing at 255 then, so I was bigger and stronger and could handle the tackles better. I also had good quickness to pull out when I had to."

There remained the championship game, this time at New York against the 8–3–1 Giants. The Bears led the league in scoring with 363 points (permitting 246), while the Giants kept their opponents under 200 points (197), one of only four of the dozen NFL teams to do so. They scored 264.

A Yankee Stadium crowd of 56,836 watched as the Giants' Gene Filipski returned the opening kickoff 53 yards to the Bears' 39. In just four more plays the Giants and Mel Triplett were in the end zone with the first score of the game. The 7–0 advantage was extended to 13–0 on a pair of Ben Agajanian field goals, and the rout was on. By halftime the score was 34–7. The Giants then put up 13 more unanswered points in the second half to win the championship by a lopsided 47–7 score. Before the game, Giants head coach Jim Lee Howell had sent two players out on the field to test the turf. One of them, Ed Hughes, slipped and fell, while the other, Gene Filipski, made his way without difficulty. Of note is that Hughes was wearing football shoes while Filipski was in basketball sneakers.

TRIVIA

Halas was 61 when he turned over his Bears to a younger Driscoll. How old was the new coach?

Answers to the trivia questions are on pages 182–183.

With that, Howell ordered his team to don basketball shoes for the contest. Although the Bears also wore shoes with rubber soles, the Giants jumped out to a 20–0 lead, and the shoes became a major postgame story.

The statistics were far less lopsided than the score, as the Bears gained only 68 fewer yards than the Giants. The difference, however, was in rushing, as the Giants held Casares (who did score the Bears' lone TD on a nine-yard run) and company to just 67 yards, gaining 126 themselves.

Bouncing Around

Bears fans had reason for optimism as 1957 approached. The team had gone 25–10–1 over the previous three seasons, capping off the three-year run with a conference title in '56. Zeke Bratkowski was back from the service, Casares was in the backfield along with rookie Willie Galimore, some of the youngsters were developing on the offensive line, while Bill George, Joe Fortunato, and back J. C. Caroline were forming a strong defense.

By the third week of the season the Bears were 0–3 and among the league's bigger disappointments. The team then rallied to win three of its next four, but a 3–4 record was not a reason for optimism. A loss to the Colts was followed by a convincing 27–7 victory over the eventual champion Detroit Lions, but that was it. Chicago dropped two of the remaining three to close the season 5–7–0.

The problem was offense, as the Bears scored 160 points fewer than in '56, while the defense actually improved by 35 points.

Halas had seen enough, and the 63-year-old owner took over as coach once again in 1958. His impact was felt immediately. Chicago opened the '58 campaign with a rousing 34–20 road win over Green Bay. The powerful Colts were just too tough in Game 2, crushing the Bears 51–38 in Baltimore. Halas tightened the defense, and the team won the next three in a row, giving up a total of just 30 points in the process. After splitting the next two, Halas readied his team for an invasion by the powerful 6–1 Colts. When Weeb Ewbank's charges prevailed 17–0, the 5–3 Bears were all but out of it. Nonetheless, Chicago reeled off three more wins to close the season with an 8–4 mark and a tie with the Rams for second in the West, one game behind the eventual champion Colts. Respectability, if not championship play, had returned.

George Halas had many reputations. One of his more notorious was his propensity for being tight-fisted, which always came into play during player contract negotiations. Bears back Johnny Morris was drafted in 1958 and signed the standard rookie contract for $6,000. Halas told him they liked him a lot and if he had a good season, the Bears "would take care of him." As Morris recalls:

Well, I had a pretty good season. I started about half the time at halfback—I kind of alternated starting with Willie Galimore—and I ran back most of the kickoffs and punts. After the season, I was called in to see Halas. I felt good; I really proved myself, I thought. I knew our talk was to be about the next year's contract.

George Blanda, shown here as a Houston Oiler in a game where he attempted 68 passes, never blossomed with the Bears but went on to a stellar NFL career.

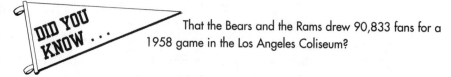

That the Bears and the Rams drew 90,833 fans for a 1958 game in the Los Angeles Coliseum?

With memories of, "You do a good job, I'll take care of you." still in my head, I was thinking maybe $10,000, $12,000, something like that. I was excited. Halas gave me that smile of his when I sat down. "You had a good year. I'm going to give you a $500 raise." I played for $6,500 in 1959.

(A Pro Bowl and All-Pro pick, Morris began as a rusher but went on to become one of the league's premier pass receivers. He was in many ways a forerunner of the possession receiver of today.)

On the flip side, Halas could be generous. Hugh Gallarneau shares his story about the time Halas surprised him with a bonus check.

George Halas, always the intelligent businessman, withheld 20 percent of your total compensation for the season so that when the season was over you'd have something to go home with. When I came in to see him at the end of the season, he mentioned the fact that for a short period of time I had tied the NFL record for touchdowns, at least until George McAfee and Don Hutson beat it that year. We settled up on the 20 percent, and then he handed me a check for $500. I said, "Well, what's that for, George?" He said, "You did have a good season: you averaged 6.2 yards a carry. For a rookie you did a damn good job. This is your bonus."

Gallarneau protested, but Halas told him to shut up and take the money. Perhaps the final say on this matter came from Mike Ditka, who once quipped that Halas "tossed nickels around like manhole covers."

The Colts were the team to beat in 1959, and the Bears set their sights on the men from Baltimore. Unfortunately, four losses in their first five games all but buried the Chicagoans early. Although the team's lone win had come against Baltimore, a loss in Game 4 meant the teams would not meet again that year. Halas, however, was not one to give up. Hoping the veteran Colts would flag down the stretch, he rode the Bears through the rest of their schedule, winning all seven games, giving the team another 8–4–0 mark. The Colts stumbled to 4–3 in midseason, but managed to win their final five to finish a length ahead at 9–3–0.

Although the club posted a creditable 70–48–2 record, the '50s closed with the Bears shut out as far as NFL championships were concerned. The team did post seven winning seasons, but claimed only one conference flag, finishing second five times.

TRIVIA

With which team did Doug Atkins finish his NFL career?

Answers to the trivia questions are on pages 182–183.

George Blanda left the Bears in 1959 at 31, because he did not want to be relegated to kicking. He was not the clearcut No. one quarterback until 1953, when he threw 363 passes for 2,163 yards. He threw for 1,929 the following year, but his 40 interceptions in those two years did not endear him to Halas, who liked Blanda better as a kicker. Blanda was as competitive as they come, however, and it extended beyond the playing field. Stan Jones said, "Blanda would bet on anything. You'd go to a bowling alley, and he'd bet he could beat you. You'd play a pinball machine, and he'd be there with a bet." He was also chronically nervous. In one tight game, Blanda lined up behind Jones, the right guard, instead of the center, and starting calling signals.

Blanda returned to the American Football League's Houston Oilers in 1960 and played until 1975, when he was 48 years old. He was in the Hall of Fame by 1981.

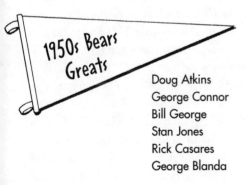

1950s Bears Greats

Doug Atkins
George Connor
Bill George
Stan Jones
Rick Casares
George Blanda

Chasing

The 1960 season began with only one NFL team left in the Windy City, the Cardinals having packed their gear and headed south to St. Louis. Moreover, the NFL expanded, adding a team. The Dallas Cowboys were planted in Texas to go head-to-head with the new American Football League's Dallas Texans. On the AFL front, Lamar Hunt, the league's founder, became its first president. The rival league received a major boost when it entered a contract with ABC to televise its games. In addition, the AFL instituted the college two-point conversion option, not available in the NFL. The teams also added the players' names to the backs of their jerseys.

Unlike 1959, the Bears broke out of the gate with a vengeance, winning three of their first four, including a season-opening 17–14 conquest of the contemptible Packers. A tie followed by a pair of losses chilled enthusiasm a tad, but after a pair of wins the team was 5–3–1, and a half game out of first place. And then the bottom inexplicably flopped out. Chicago lost to Green Bay, Cleveland, and Detroit by a combined 119–13 score, closing the books on 1960 with a 5–6–1 mark. Even worse, the Bears were once again chasing Green Bay—back in the business of battling for league supremacy.

Things were better in '61, with the Bears at 5–2 in midseason. The team did drop three straight from there—against Philadelphia, Green Bay, and San Francisco, teams that would go a combined 28–13–1—but then righted the ship, winning three of the final four to finish at 8–6–0 in the now 14-game schedule. Despite the better record, the Bears were nonfactors in the Western Conference, as Green Bay won 11 of 14 and went on to demolish the Giants 37–0 in the championship game. On the plus side, however, Bill Wade, whom Halas had gotten from Los Angeles

DID YOU KNOW . . . That in 1961 the 49ers were much the rage operating out of the shotgun formation, only to have the Bears—led by middle linebacker Bill George—scuttle the novel formation to the tune of 31–0? San Francisco then returned to a more conventional offense.

to run the offense, ranked fifth in passing, and rookie tight end Mike Ditka, from Pitt, was fifth in receiving with 56 receptions.

Prior to Ditka the tight end was simply one more interior lineman. He just happened to be lined up at the end of that string of blockers. Ditka was nothing less than a ferocious blocker, but in addition, helped turn the position into one that included pass receiving as well. An absolutely dominant player as an All-American at Pittsburgh, Ditka was not only the league's rookie of the year in 1961, he was All-NFL from 1961 to 1964 and a member of the Pro Bowl squad from '61 to '65. Called "Iron Mike," Ditka did not miss a start in 84 games with Chicago. He averaged 53 catches a year from 1961 to 1966, numbers that look as if they came from a more contemporary era in which the tight end is primarily a pass receiver. His numbers continued to grow until injuries started beating him down.

By 1962, despite some struggling franchises, the AFL was showing no signs of going away. Moreover, NFL owners were having to dust off their checkbooks, as locking up college talent was becoming a more expensive venture with two leagues competing for the same players. On the NFL gridiron it was pretty much all Green Bay all the time in 1962, as the defending champion Packers came within a single game of going undefeated, 13–1. They manhandled the Bears twice by a combined 87–7. Aside from the embarrassments handed out by the Packers, Halas's team acquitted itself very nicely in '62, going 9–3 against the rest of the league, good enough for third in the now seven-team West. Ditka and Johnny Morris each caught 58 passes.

Halas was many things, but there was one thing he was not: a quitter. The 68-year-old coach was simply not going to give up the chase of Lombardi's Green Bay Packers. So the campaign to catch the Pack resumed in 1963. In Green Bay, however, the goal was

TRIVIA

Which Bears assistant put together a zone defense that was a key to the success of the 1963 team?

Answers to the trivia questions are on pages 182–183.

Challenge III—the quest to win a third straight NFL championship, an accomplishment that barely eluded Halas on two occasions.

The season opened with a stunner. The Bears beat the Packers 10–3 in Green Bay. Four games later the team was 5–0, a game ahead of Green Bay. A 20–14 loss in San Francisco the next week, however, pulled Chicago back into a tie with the Pack. After nine games the teams were still deadlocked at 8–1 and ready to meet in Chicago to settle matters the next week. Settle them they did, as the Bears pummeled Green Bay by a convincing 26–7 score. Chicago then suffered an apparent letdown, managing only ties against Pittsburgh and Minnesota, but then won their final two contests to close the 1963 books at 11–1–2. The Packers could hardly have come closer, going 11–2–1. Nonetheless, the chase was over, and the Bears ruled the West. It could hardly be sweeter. Defense was the key, as the team allowed a puny 144 points in 14 games—62 points better than No. 2 Green Bay—scoring 301. The Packers put up 369, but allowed 206.

For Bears tight end Mike Ditka the 1963 season was the highlight of his playing career with the Bears. "Our finest season, of course, was 1963. The first thing I remember about that season was when we played the Giants in the preseason. We beat them, and after the game Coach Halas called me in and asked me about where I thought we could go that year. I said I thought we could win it all. ... The game in Pittsburgh was memorable. The play that everybody seems to remember about me was in the Steelers game that year." Ditka took a short pass and ran 63 yards, breaking at least five tackles to set up the game-tying field goal. "I don't really know that it was the best," he says, "because if it had been the best play I ever made, I would have scored a touchdown, and I would have outrun that last guy."

TRIVIA

Mike Ditka was a first-year player without peer in 1961, but the Bears also had a young 1962 star who was Rookie of the Year. Who was he?

Answers to the trivia questions are on pages 182–183.

Bears quarterback Bill Wade has another memory of that game. "I'll never forget going to Pittsburgh the weekend after President Kennedy's assassination. We didn't know whether we were going to play a game that Sunday or not. We did. And Coach Halas got the whole team together before it and told us we were going to go out there and play and hope we can get everybody's mind off the terrible tragedy. It was a very depressing situation."

There was still the NFL championship tussle on the schedule. This would pit Chicago against the New York Giants, a Y. A. Tittle–led offensive machine that ran up 448 points, a 32-points-per-game average. With the Chicago temperature at 11 degrees, 45,801 fans piled into Wrigley Field on December 29. The Bears, in a near frenzy, tore into the Giants, intercepting five Tittle passes and battering the quarterback unmercifully. The scoring actually began with a New York score, in which Frank Gifford caught a 14-yard pass for a touchdown. Wade evened things up on a two-yard plunge, but a Don Chandler field goal put New York up 10–3 at the half.

That, however, was it for the Giants, but the Bears and Billy Wade managed one more TD on a one-yard score by Wade, and the championship belonged to Chicago, 14–10. Johnny Morris credits the defense for leading the Bears that year and in the championship game, "It was the defense that year that got us to the title game against the Giants, and it

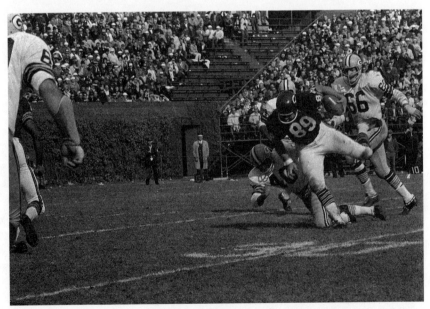

Mike Ditka, here making a catch against the Packers in 1966, revolutionized the tight end position.

By the
NUMBERS

Rick Casares by the Numbers

Casares was the backbone of the Bears' ground game for much of his career. A Floridian who went to the University of Florida, the powerful running back had an immediate impact on the Bears in an era in which the ground game dominated. A five-time Pro Bowl selection, Casares led the NFL in rushing by more than 200 yards in 1956.

Yr.	Gms.	R.Att.	Ydg.	Avg.	TDs
1955	12	125	672	5.4	4
1956	12	234	1,126	4.8	12
1957	12	204	700	3.4	6
1958	12	176	651	3.7	2
1959	12	177	699	3.9	10
1960	12	160	566	3.5	5
1961	13	135	588	4.4	8
1962	13	75	255	3.4	2
1963	10	65	277	4.3	0
1964	13	35	123	3.5	0
	121	1,386	5,657	4.1	49

was the defense who won that game for us. They were awesome in 1963." The 1963 defense lauded by Morris consisted of Doug Atkins, Ed O'Bradovich, Stan Jones, Fred Williams, Bill George, Joe Fortunato, Larry Morris (who won the championship game MVP), Richie Petitbon, Rosey Taylor, Bennie McRae, and Davey Whitsell.

Special teams play was also instrumental in the championship game, especially the play of J. C. Caroline. Morris again: "[Caroline] had the greatest game I've ever seen of a guy on special teams that day. When we watched the films of the game, watched him making tackle after tackle, everybody was overwhelmed. When the film was finally turned off, somebody said his name, and everybody in the room gave him a spontaneous ovation. Here were 40 hard-nosed guys just wrapped up in their emotions watching what he did in that game and just breaking into an ovation. That was really something." As was the 1963 season.

Tough Times

Were Halas and the Bears going to reestablish hegemony in the NFL, as they had decades ago, or were the Packers going to restore order in 1964 under Lombardi?

Strangely neither the Bears nor the Packers were genuine factors in the 1964 race. The 12–2 Baltimore Colts ran away with the West, while the Packers were only good enough for an 8–5–1 record. The Bears encountered a string of season-destroying injuries to the likes of Doug Atkins, defensive end Ed O'Bradovich, and linebacker Bill George, among others. Johnny Morris did set a league mark with 93 pass receptions, while Mike Ditka snagged 75 more, but the team could do no better than a 5–9–0 log. Injuries really curtailed the defense as Chicago yielded nearly 17 points per game more than in championship '63.

Tragedy struck the Bears training camp in 1964. Running back Willie Galimore, an elusive running back who had been with the team since 1957, and John "Bo" Farrington, an end since 1960, were killed in an automobile accident near the team's Rensselaer, Indiana, training camp.

Off the field, the NFL signed a lucrative TV pact with CBS, but the AFL nearly matched it on NBC. The war between the leagues would continue, and the AFL with its high-scoring style of wide-open play was putting down roots.

The big news in 1965 was the signing of the $400,000 plum, quarterback Joe Namath of the Alabama Crimson Tide, by the New York Jets of the AFL. Moreover, both the NFL and AFL expanded with an NFL franchise in Atlanta and an AFL counterpart in Miami, both to begin play in 1966.

There were two reasons the Bears rebounded with a 9–5–0 mark in '65, third behind Baltimore and Green Bay at 10–3–1: Dick Butkus and Gale Sayers. Perhaps never before or since has one team drafted a pair of

No one in Bears history was fiercer or more intimidating than Bears linebacker Dick Butkus, here making an impressive open-field tackle of the Packers' John Brockington in 1972.

this stature—both All-Pro in their rookie years and both eventual members of the Pro Football Hall of Fame.

No player was more electrifying that the "Kansas Comet," a 1964 All-American out of the Great Plains, in his healthy years. Sayers was so incredible that he was inducted into the Hall of Fame on the strength of essentially five years of professional football. Butkus is to linebackers what Jim Brown is to running backs—the standard by which players of his era were measured.

The season started out abysmally, with losses in San Francisco, Los Angeles, and Green Bay. Then came nine wins in 10 games to drive the team's record to 9–4–0. A 24–17 loss to Minnesota in the finale left the team at 9–5–0. The team improved its scoring acumen by nearly 11 points a game as Sayers came in second in rushing and Rudy Bukich led the league in passing. Sayers also scored 22 touchdowns that year, including a record six in one game against San Francisco.

Sayers was the show in 1966, leading the NFL in rushing and kickoff returns, as well as catching 34 passes in a year in which receiver Morris was out much of the time with a knee injury. Nonetheless, the offense foundered as Chicago averaged less than 17 points per game and finished a poor 5–7–2.

Assistant Coach George Allen, still under contract with the Bears, opted to leave the Bears to coach the Los Angeles Rams in 1966, but he did do without Halas's permission. Halas tried to prevent Allen from leaving, with the dispute ending up in court. Halas actually won in court, then stunned the gathered throng by releasing Allen to go Los Angeles, feeling he had accomplished his objective, that of proving that an assistant under contract cannot simply leave after receiving a better offer. Curiously enough, Allen went on to become a Hall of Fame coach, though he never won an NFL title.

On the plus side, a merger agreement was struck with the American Football League, ending the expensive war. A Super Bowl would be played at the end of the season, matching the AFL and NFL champion, but far more reassuring for both sets of owners, a common draft would begin in 1967. The new structure would have 26 teams by '68 and would begin playing as one league in 1970, with Pete Rozelle as the sole commissioner.

By 1967 the Packers were again going for their third straight NFL championship, while the Bears were trying to emerge from tough times and establish a consistent winning record. Now in the Central Division of the Western Conference—the NFL having expanded to 16 teams with the addition of the New Orleans Saints— the Bears battled and scratched to a 5–1–1 finishing kick to post a still ho-hum 7–6–1 record.

That was enough for Halas, as the 73-year-old retired from coaching for the

TRIVIA

In 1968, after the Bears lost their top two quarterbacks, who stepped in and guided them to four straight wins before breaking a leg himself?

Answers to the trivia questions are on pages 182–183.

All-Time Bears

Receivers (listed alphabetically)

Marty Booker—Five-year Bear and Pro Bowl invitee in 2002, caught 197 passes for more than 2,200 yards in '01 and '02.

Curtis Conway—Averaged 47 catches a season over seven years ('93–'99), scoring 31 TDs.

Mike Ditka—Hall of Fame tight end who led the Bears in receiving for three years and was a Pro Bowl pick each of his first five years, starting in 1961.

Jim Dooley—Eight years a Bear in the rushing-oriented '50s and early '60s, cleared the 500-yard mark in receiving yards four times, reaching 841 on 53 catches in 1953; second to Johnny Morris in all-time receiving yards.

Willie Gault—Deep threat from '83 to '87 for the Bears, scoring 27 TDs, the Bears' top receiver each year.

Dick Gordon—Seven years a Bear, twice a Pro Bowl selection, and topping the league in receptions and receiving TDs in 1970.

Harlon Hill—Pro Bowl pick in each of his first three years ('54–'56), twice over the thousand mark in receiving yards in a season and twice led NFL in TD receptions.

Ken Kavanaugh—Scored 50 TDs through the air in his eight-year career with the Bears, playing on three NFL championship teams.

Johnny Morris—Caught 356 passes in his 10-year career, leading the NFL with 93 catches in Pro Bowl 1964 season when he gained 1,200 yards and scored 10 TDs, both totals also league leaders.

Marcus Robinson—Twice the Bears' No. 1 receiver; caught 84 passes for 1,400 yards in 1999.

last time. His record was 324–151–31, a mark that at the time appeared impossible to surpass.

TRIVIA

Who did the Bears get from the Eagles in 1967 in exchange for Ditka?

Answers to the trivia questions are on pages 182–183.

The new coach was an old face, Jim Dooley, who had been with Halas as a player and coach since 1952. Dooley lost his first two games and then two of the next three, before reeling off four straight wins. Tragedy struck, however, in Game 9 when the great Gale Sayers tore up his right knee at home against the 49ers and was gone for the season. It turned out to be a 7–7–0 season, one in which the Bears yielded 83 more points than they scored.

The 1969 season was one of some highs and many lows. On the high side, Sayers returned to lead the league in rushing with 1,032 yards on 236 carries. On the low end, the Bears suffered their worst season, going 1–13–0. Six of the losses were by six points or less.

A less than sterling decade was over, one in which Chicago was just a barely-over-.500 franchise, at 67–65–6. There had been one championship early (1963), but only five winning seasons against four losers and one 7–7–0 campaign. Moreover, for the first time in many years the future did not look bright for the Bears. They had finished out of the money for six straight years, and with Halas gone and the 1963 championship campaign a distant memory, they showed no sign of a return to gridiron prominence.

"I Love Brian Piccolo"

He didn't get any lifetime achievement award, an honor rooted in the cumulative weight of a lengthy career's statistics. No, Gale Sayers played the equivalent of five years, but was so spectacular in that short time frame that he went straight from the playing field into the Hall of Fame.

Rosey Grier, an All-Pro defensive tackle with the Rams in 1965, liked to describe the time he hit Gale Sayers with what he thought was a ball-jarring hit. Many of this cohorts on defense throughout the league no doubt had similar stories. "I hit him so hard, I thought my shoulder must have busted him in two. I heard a roar from the crowd and figured he had fumbled. Then there he was 15 yards down the field heading for the end zone."

No game is more representative of the Kansas Comet's brilliance than his performance in the December mud of Wrigley Field in a game against the San Francisco 49ers. Chased all over the field, Sayers motored into the end zone again and again. By the fourth touchdown fans were ruminating about what the record for TDs in a game was and what additional wonders Gale would wreak. The additional wonders included two more scores, for a record-setting six touchdowns in a single game. "The six touchdowns I saw Gale Sayers score is the greatest feat I have ever witnessed," wrote Donald Mankin in *The Coffin Corner.*

"After the sixth touchdown the place went up for grabs," noted Mankin.

But here is the real stunner. Sayers could well have powered in once more. He was on the field late in the game when Jon Arnett plunged a yard for the team's final touchdown. As Sayers later said:

The way things were going I probably could have scored eight touchdowns that day. But back then no one cared about records,

DID YOU KNOW . . . That Piccolo is one of only two non–Hall of Fame Bears whose numbers have been retired?

and no one kept track of them. I didn't even know I'd tied the six-touchdown record until after the ballgame. Today they have people in the press box with record books, and they're always announcing that this player needs one more fumble to do this, or that player needs to complete one more pass to do that. We were ahead by 40 points, we had the game, so who cared about scoring seven or eight touchdowns? We won the ballgame, and that was the most important thing at that time.

There are some players whose performances are so beyond the norm that they are unable to be described effectively. Gale Sayers was one of those players. His incredible zigzagging running style was unique and breathtaking. He looked as if he had the trunk of a man's body perfectly attached to large bicycle wheels. And how those wheels could turn and cut.

Despite his singular gridiron brilliance, Sayers is known by many as the roommate and best friend of the late Brian Piccolo. In an era of overt racial tension and at best contrived desegregation, the white Piccolo and the black Sayers voluntarily roomed together, even though they each played running back and were, in a sense, competitors for playing time.

When Sayers was injured in 1968, Piccolo stepped in and averaged 90 yards a game in the final five contests of the season. It was Piccolo, however, who during the off-season following Sayers severe right knee injury encouraged and worked out with the Comet to help bring him back to greatness, a greatness that would cost Piccolo playing time. Sayers, much due to Piccolo's urging and companionship, did make it back, leading the league in rushing in 1969.

In November of 1969, Piccolo took himself out of a game because of difficulties with breathing. Having had a nagging cough for some time, he was given a chest X-ray only to discover he had a huge tumor in his chest. He was

TRIVIA

The popular book about Piccolo's life and battle with cancer was titled *Brian Piccolo: A Short Season*. Who was its author?

Answers to the trivia questions are on pages 182–183.

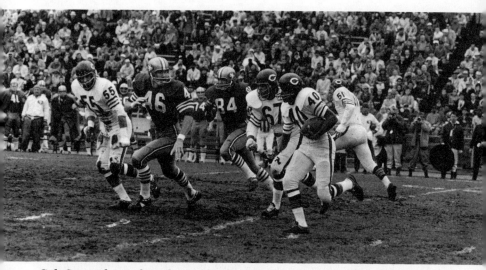

Gale Sayers, here taking the opening kickoff 97 yards for a touchdown against San Francisco in 1967, was the most gifted and electric back in Bears history. Two years earlier he scored six touchdowns in one game against the same opponent.

operated upon on November 28, 1969, with the physicians optimistic about its results. Piccolo began working out shortly after recovering from the surgery, intending to play in 1970.

Bears linebacker Doug Buffone remembers: "We had a basketball team when the season was over. Traveled all over. Pic [Piccolo] couldn't play anymore, so we made him our coach. Then, after one of the games, Pic said to me that he thought he felt a lump or something in his chest. So back to the hospital he went. Then it was really over. We all knew things weren't going well the second time he went to the hospital. When we'd talk about it, Sayers would say, 'Well, give him a holler; it'll pick him up.' And usually when you did call him he'd say, 'Yeah, everything's fine.'"

A few weeks later the physicians determined the only hope to save Piccolo's life was to remove his left lung. On April 9, 1970, Piccolo's lung was removed with radiation to follow. It was unsuccessful. Game to the end, Sayers's best friend—the cheerful, kind, and courageous Brian Piccolo—lost his life on June 16, 1970, leaving his wife, Joy, and their three daughters, women he loved intensely, as his survivors. The Bible says God never sends trouble to anyone in excess of what the person can handle. Brian Piccolo showed what he was made of in his gracious handling of a burden that would simply break the spirit of many lesser souls.

For Sayers, knowing Brian—a man who took time to speak to seriously ill children about keeping a positive outlook when his own life was in the balance—was life changing. With Piccolo close to the end in May of 1970,

TRIVIA

Which university did Piccolo attend?

Answers to the trivia questions are on pages 182–183.

Sayers, upon receiving the NFL's Most Courageous Player award for his Piccolo-aided comeback from a devastated knee, had this to say to the crowd. "I love Brian Piccolo, and I'd like all of you to love him. When you hit your knees to pray tonight, please ask God to love him, too."

For the great Gale Sayers, the road ahead proved steep professionally. A left knee injury in 1970 slowed his career to a near stop, and it was over for him as an NFL player by 1971. Nonetheless, no one who ever saw the Kansas Comet run, in person or even on film, will likely ever forget the greatness of Gale Sayers. We will never see his likeness again.

Sayers and Piccolo by the Numbers

Sayers's stats are just eye-popping and revealing. They are eye-popping when you look at his kickoff-return averages in his early, healthy years. They are revealing in that his elusiveness screams out from the numbers. Moreover, though not used largely as a pass receiver, Gale snared 112 passes for 1,307 yards and nine touchdowns.

Yr.	Gms.	R.A.	R.Yd.	Avg.	TD	K.R.	Ydg.	Avg.	TD
1965	14	166	867	5.2	14	21	660	31.4	1
1966	14	229	1,231	5.4	8	23	718	32.1	2
1967	13	186	880	4.7	7	16	603	37.7	3
1968	9	138	856	6.2	2	17	461	27.1	0
1969	14	236	1,032	4.4	8	14	339	24.2	0
1970	2	23	52	2.3	0	0	0	0.0	0
1971	2	13	38	2.9	0	0	0	0.0	0
	68	991	4,956	5.0	39	91	2,781	30.6	6

The numbers of Piccolo are modest. He played in 51 games, rushed 258 times for 927 yards—an average of 3.6—and four touchdowns. He caught 58 passes for 537 yards, a 9.3 average, and one TD. Numbers, however, can never tell what a champion Piccolo was beyond the game.

Linebacker, Inc.

By the 1960s the Bears' identity had been firmly established. A Halas-owned—and especially coached—squad would be long on physicality and short on finesse, competent on offense, and super-tough on defense. A key to the vaunted 1963 Chicago defense, one that parted with just 10.3 points per game, was its incredible linebacker play. With Bill George in the middle and Joe Fortunato and Larry Morris on the outside, the Bears had a hangman's defensive dragnet.

Of the three, Bill George was the most renowned. A graduate of Wake Forest, the 6'2" 230-pounder had been an All-American tackle in college. Picked in the second round in 1951, George immediately was moved to the middle guard position in the then-common five-man front of the 1950s. In a 1954 game with the Eagles, the Bears put a wrinkle in their defense. George had been instructed to bump the center at the snap and then drop back to defend against the pass. It wasn't effective as the Eagles were completing short throws over George. "I could break up those passes," George said to Bears star George Connor, "if I didn't have to hit that offensive center first."

"What are you hitting him for, then?" Connor retorted, "Why don't you go for the ball?"

The very next pass hit George in the stomach. Next he snared the first of his 18 career interceptions. The new twist caught on, and by 1957 the wire services omitted the middle guard position on All-Pro teams and inserted a middle linebacker instead. As for George, he was already a star. Named All-Pro at middle guard in 1955 and '56, he was dubbed all-league middle linebacker in 1957. By 1963 the Bears' man in the middle was given All-Pro honors for the eighth time.

DID YOU KNOW . . . That of Fortunato, George, Butkus, Connor, and Singletary, George was the only player who did not play his entire career in a Bears uniform?

George had quite a year in 1954, adding 25 points on 13 PATs and four field goals to his defensive heroics.

"Bill George was the first great middle linebacker," said later Bears head coach Abe Gibron. "He brought all the romance and charisma to the position. He was like having Clark Shaughnessy [the Bears revered defensive coach] on the field. He called all the plays and had special knack for it."

Part of that knack was the controversial practice of timing his calls to the cadence of the opposing quarterback.

"You've got to put constant pressure on the good quarterbacks," George noted in a before-his-time comment. "One time, we went into a three-man line with eight players in the secondary to face Johnny Unitas and he still picked us to pieces. You just can't let the good quarterbacks get set."

Extremely tough, George played the '62 season in intense pain, owing to severe neck damage between the fifth and sixth vertebra from an automobile accident after the 1961 season.

On November 1, 1964, the big Syrian was given a day in his honor at Wrigley Field only to sustain a severe knee injury early in the game. He missed the last six games of the season, the first time the 15-year veteran (13 as a Bear) and eight-time Pro Bowler had been out of a game due to injury.

George was inducted into the Hall of Fame in 1974. Although the Bears great died in 1982 at just 53, he lives on through the Bill George Youth Football League program, named in his honor.

To Bill George's left stood former Mississippi State fullback Joe Fortunato, at outside linebacker. Though overshadowed by George, Fortunato—who arrived in Chicago in 1955—carved a memorable profile in the Bears' defense, good enough to be named to the '63 All-Pro squad. The fierce-tackling Fortunato was named to five Pro Bowl squads and three All-Pro teams during his career and gave opposing quarterbacks little relief, should they choose to stay away from the middle and head to Joe's side of the field.

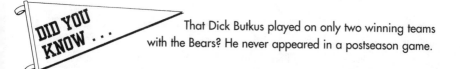

That Dick Butkus played on only two winning teams with the Bears? He never appeared in a postseason game.

On the right was Larry Morris from Georgia Tech who joined the team beginning in the 1959 season after three seasons with the Rams. Though he was never as celebrated as George or Fortunato, teams were unwise to believe that Morris was a soft touch. Y. A. Tittle, who fired 36 TD strikes during the regular season, found that out in the '63 title game when it was Morris who dominated the championship contest. He racked up Tittle's knee with a second-quarter tackle and then picked off one of the Hall of Famer's passes, setting up the Bears' first TD with a 61-yard return.

But these were only three linebackers in the great tradition of linebacking that is the Bears. The previously mentioned George Connor all but defined the position during his eight years with Chicago. A Hall of Fame member, Connor did not begin his career as a linebacker. He was an especially mobile tackle, but when the great Steve Van Buren became all but unstoppable on end sweeps, the Bears inserted the agile Connor to counter Van Buren and his blockers. He did, and a superstar linebacker was born.

Connor was renowned for his intellect, sniffing out plays by reading keys even before the practice was common. There is no way of determining how great he may have become had a knee injury not halted his career at 30 years of age.

Nearly three decades later, Mike Singletary carried on the tradition of Bears linebacking greats. An incredibly hard hitter and brilliant tactician, Singletary was a coach on the field directing the Bears' awesome 46 Defense. Only a second-round draft pick in 1981, and considered too small by many, the 6'0", 230-pound Singletary started 172 straight games. He was twice the NFL Defensive Player of the Year, eight times All-Pro, and a member of 10 Pro Bowl squads.

Despite his devout, almost ministerial character, Singletary was involved in a near reverse parent-child relationship with the often unhinged Ditka. Despite his balanced character, however, the linebacker embodied intensity. He played with bulging eyes, giving him a deranged, obsessive look, but all this belied "Samurai's" calculating ability to focus on the offense and stop it cold.

Mike Singletary simply loved the game. "Do you know what my favorite part of the game is?" he would ask. "The opportunity to play."

But when you talk about Bears linebackers, one name is separated from all the rest. That name is Dick Butkus. Butkus—his very name is hard, linebacker-like. His number was 51, and his job was legalized mayhem. He intimidated opponents. "If I had a choice, I would rather go one-on-one with a grizzly bear," said former Packers back MacArthur Lane. "I prayed that I could get up every time Butkus hit me."

A stalwart of the Bears defenses of the early 1960s, Bill George was inducted into the Pro Football Hall of Fame in 1974.

The 6'3", 245-pound Butkus would work himself into a frenzy before a game. "When I went out on the field to warm up," he recalled, "I would manufacture things to make me mad. If someone on the other team was laughing, I'd pretend he was laughing at me or the Bears. I'd find something to get mad about. It always worked for me." He wanted to be a pro football player when he was in grade school and read that the key was being tough, very tough.

As a rookie, Butkus made an immediate impression on Hall of Fame great Bill George. "The second I saw him on the field," said George, "I knew my playing days were over. Nobody ever looked that good before or since."

A six-time All-Pro—including his rookie year—and seven times on the Pro Bowl squad, like Connor, Butkus's career was over at 30 with a knee injury.

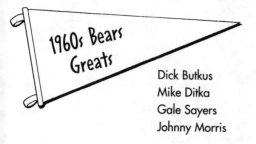

1960s Bears Greats

Dick Butkus
Mike Ditka
Gale Sayers
Johnny Morris

Forgotten Years

The new decade brought a complete realignment of 26 now NFL-only franchises. No longer were there American and National Football Leagues. Instead there was one NFL with an American and National Conference. Pete Rozelle had continued to impress and was now very secure in the commissioner's chair. As for the new structure, each conference had three divisions. The Bears were members of the NFC Central, along with Minnesota, Detroit, and Green Bay.

The NFL was now truly big league. Many date the emergence of the NFL into the national consciousness to the remarkable sudden-death NFL title game in New York in 1958 when the Colts prevailed against the Giants, 23–17. Ever since Alan Ameche rumbled into the end zone the NFL gained momentum as a major source of entertainment. By 1970 baseball was in eclipse, bogged down by slow-moving, low-scoring games, while the NFL was providing thrills every week.

For Bears fans it was all bittersweet. The team was coming off the worst season in its history. Little did they know that they would wait well into the '70s before a glimmer of worthy hope would appear.

That the Bears won even six of 14 games during the 1970 season is surprising. After the pain of losing Piccolo to cancer, the team watched Gale Sayers hurt his right knee in preseason. After winning the first two against the Giants and the Eagles, the team dropped four straight. Promising quarterback Bobby Douglass, after winning Game 10 with four touchdown passes against Buffalo (giving Chicago a 4–6 mark), broke his ankle and was gone for the final four contests. Some consolation was gained by defeating Green Bay, 35–17, in the Bears' final game in Wrigley Field on December 13. They would move to monstrous Soldier Field for the 1971 season.

TOP TEN

Worst Bears Seasons

1. 1969 (1–13–0)—Won only against fellow 1–13 team, the Pittsburgh Steelers.
2. 1975 (4–10–0)—Was minus-188 in net points and placed 24th and 19th in total offense and defense, respectively, among league's 26 franchises.
3. 2002 (4–12–0)—Ranked 29th in offense and 25th in defense among 32 NFL teams.
4. 1997 (4–12–0)—Was outscored by 158 points in the first of two straight dismal campaigns.
5. 1973 (3–11–0)—Was outscored by 139 points in 14 games.
6. 1998 (4–12–0)—Was 25th in points scored and 23rd in points permitted in the 30-team league.
7. 1974 (4–10–0)—Ranked 25th among 26 teams in total offense.
8. 2000 (5–11–0)—Was 24th on offense and 16th on defense in a year in which the team was outscored by 139 points.
9. 2004 (5–11–0)—Was last in total offense and 21st on defense while yielding 100 more points than the team scored.
10. 1964 (5–9–0)—Was beaten by a net 119 points.

The new venue proved rather favorable for the Bears as the 1971 team was 5–2 after seven games, despite Sayers's inability to return from his knee woes. Kent Nix, out of Texas Christian, was all the rage after some early wins. Soon, however, he and Jack Concannon were out with injuries, and the quarterback job reverted to Bobby Douglass. When the Bears dropped six of their last seven, Dooley was out as coach with a 20–36–0 record after four years.

The 1972 season was a perfect one for the Miami Dolphins, as the Florida entry roared through its 14-game regular-season schedule without a defeat and then made it a spotless 17–0 by defeating George Allen and his Washington team in Super Bowl VII, 14–7. It was not at all perfect for the Bears and new coach Abe Gibron, another Halas loyalist.

With Sayers now retired, Gibron turned to Bobby Douglass, who generated offense in a most unusual way. Repeatedly he would go back into the pocket to pass, but at the seeming first opportunity blow out of the pocket and

TRIVIA

What did Cecil Turner do to excite fans in 1970?

Answers to the trivia questions are on pages 182–183.

run like a halfback. The husky, athletic quarterback completed only 38 percent of his passes, but ran for 968 yards. The team finished 4–9–1 and placed fourth-to-last in points scored in the NFC.

After three years of the new decade, the Bears' mark was an un-Halas-like 16–25–1. With Sayers gone, no solid player under center, and the franchise's greatest coach 77 years of age, well past taking this over on the sideline, the outlook was bleak.

Things got so bad for the Bears offense during the Gibron years that one newspaperman, in noting a coach's statement that one of the injured Bears quarterbacks would be used only for holding after touchdowns, inserted the phrase, "Pause here for laughter," in reference to the rareness of a Bears touchdown, hence rarely necessitating a holder.

The sky brightened a tad in '73 when Wally Chambers, from Eastern Kentucky, caught the NFL by storm on defense. By midseason the Bobby Douglass experiment was scrapped, and the team went for a more conventional quarterback, Gary Huff. Huff, however, was a rookie and not at all ready to lead an NFL team to victory. The Bears closed the books at 3–11, managing a paltry 195 points in their 14 games—less than 14 points a game.

The following season—with both Sayers and Butkus now retired—it was pretty much the same, a 4–10–0 mark, only this time scoring just 152 points in a very different NFL. The league

Abe Gibron struggled as head coach of the Bears in the 1970s.

decided to end the incentive to tie by instituting a sudden-death overtime system for the regular as well as postseason games. In addition, the
goalposts were moved to the rear of the end zone as an added impetus
for teams to go for six rather than an easy three points.

The team had hit bottom, and Halas had had enough. He brought in
front-office wizard Jim Finks to take over all football operations. Finks
let Gibron (11–30–1) go at the end of the season and brought in Jack
Pardee as his coach.

Hiring Finks was a bold stroke by the 79-year-old owner. Finks was
from outside the organization, not a member of the Bears family. He had
been a mediocre player in the league
from 1949 to 1955 at quarterback and
defensive back for Pittsburgh. Finks,
however, had the credentials. After his
career he took over in the front office of
the expansion Minnesota Vikings and
shaped the franchise into a Super Bowl
team. It was Finks who brought an
obscure figure, a man named Bud Grant, out of Canada to coach the
Vikings.

TRIVIA

**What did Bobby Douglass
have in common with Gale
Sayers as a collegian?**

Answers to the trivia questions are on pages 182–183.

The bad news in 1975 was that the Bears had another 4–10 season.
The good news is that there was a new, competent coach, a strong football front-office man, and a brilliant young running back named Walter
Payton, all on the Bears' side. As immediate as Payton's impact was, the
behind-the-scenes maneuvering of Finks was a wonder for many to
behold. In 1976 he moved 76 players out of the organization who had
been under contract to the team. Obviously something had to be done,
and quickly. The team had been a ghastly 28–69–1 over the previous
seven seasons and 27–56–1 in the '70s. Help was on the way, however,
and the positive effects of Finks's moves were soon to be felt. The forgotten years would soon be over.

On the Road Back

The 1976 campaign opened with another sigh of relief on the part of the NFL owners. Another new enterprise, the World Football League, ran out of money and suspended operations during the '75 season. The NFL was without a rival as the 1976 season opened. Moreover, two new franchises were established, one in Tampa Bay, Florida, and the other in Seattle. Pardee's Bears started quickly with a pair of wins over the Lions at home and the 49ers on the road. The 2–0 Bears were sparking some much-needed enthusiasm around the Windy City. A 10–0 loss to Atlanta was followed by a 33–7 drubbing of Washington. Now the team was 3–1. Just when things looked the brightest Chicago took three in the teeth, to Minnesota, Los Angeles, and Dallas, all on the road. The playoffs looked a long way away.

The Bears split the next two, including a maddening 28–27 loss to the eventual Super Bowl champion Raiders, and faced their final three games with a 5–6 log. Wonder of wonders, a pair of wins over the Packers and Seahawks put the Bruins over .500 at 7–6. Despite a season-ending loss to Denver at Soldier Field, hope was on the rise in Chicago. The team was finally on the plus side in net points (253–216). Young Walter Payton was looking like the real thing as the second-year man led the conference in rushing with 1,390 yards. Less elusive than the great Sayers, "Sweetness" was powerful and injury-resistant.

In 1977 it was a tale of two seasons. Amid high hopes—fueled in part by the addition of quarterback Mike Phipps from the Cleveland Browns—it looked like the same old Bears early, as they lost two of their first three, and struggled to a 3–5 record, getting blown out 47–0 by the Houston Oilers in the eighth game. Fans were crawling off the bandwagon, not wanting to get emotionally injured in what figured to be a certain crash.

Just when things looked darkest, however, the football sky lit up. It started with a one-point win over the Kansas City Chiefs. After trailing 17–0 in what looked like a reprise of the 47–0 drubbing by Houston, Chicago put on a furious rally to bail the game out, 28–27. Then came a three-point triumph over the Vikings, in which Payton rushed for a then-record 275 yards, and a 17-point verdict over the Lions in Detroit. Suddenly the Bears were 6–5 and still in the playoff hunt, albeit a long shot. A less than impressive 10–0 win over the expansion Buccaneers and a 21–10 win over Green Bay put the team at a surprising 8–5, with a five-game winning streak.

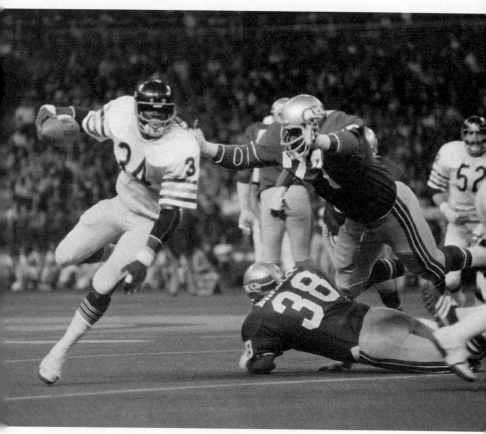

Walter Payton, here shown doing what he did best in a game against Seattle in 1976, was the first building block for what would become the great Bears teams of the mid 1980s.

1970s Bears Greats

Dick Butkus—Butkus lasted until 1972, another All-Pro season despite playing out his career with a badly battered body. His greatness was overshadowed by the sorry nature of the teams for which he played.

Walter Payton—Few players soared to brilliance faster and more consistently than "Sweetness," who took over for Rick Casares as the team's all-time rushing leader early in 1979, only his fifth season.

The streak set up a must-win against the 5–8 New York Giants on the final week of the season to crawl into the postseason as a wild-card entrant. The Giants clearly wanted to be 6–8 rather than 5–9 as they battled the Bears evenly for 60 minutes in adverse weather at Giants Stadium. The game went to overtime, and the teams struggled on for 14 minutes. If a full quarter were to pass without a score, a tie would be declared and the Bears—with Washington winning their game and posting a 9–5 mark—would have the consolation of their first winning season in a decade, but all the while realizing they had let a wild-card playoff opportunity slip through their fingers. There were nine seconds left when Bob Thomas delivered a clutch 28-yard field goal for a 12–9 win, to put Chicago in the postseason for the first time since 1963. The city went wild.

Doug Buffone remembers that game well:

We're just going back and forth, back and forth with the Giants. They're running their fullback, Larry Csonka; we're running our fullback, Robin Earl. So finally we get down close enough to kick a field goal that would win it for us. I'll never forget. Thomas came on the field. He had missed two earlier in overtime. I played on the outside end with Bob Parsons to block for the field goal. Just before the snap Parsons turns around to Thomas and says, "You better not miss this one." When he said that, I though I'd die. You know kickers are a little strange anyway. And here Bobby's got all this pressure on him, and Parsons turns around and says that. Maybe it loosened Bobby up; maybe it scared him.

All-Time Bears

Defensive Linemen (listed alphabetically)

Doug Atkins—Member of All-Pro squad of the 1960s, the Hall of Fame end was three times All-Pro and an eight-time Pro Bowl selection.

Wally Chambers—For several years in the mid-1970s, the 1973 Rookie of the Year and All-Pro tackle (and end) was a defensive dynamo during a dark period in Bears history.

Richard Dent—Four-time Pro Bowl pick, the end was, along with Dan Hampton, the backbone of the powerful Bears line of the 1980s; MVP of Super Bowl XX.

Danny Fortmann—Both-ways star at guard, was small for a lineman at 6'0", 207 pounds. The brainy Phi Beta Kappa future physician was among the elite linemen for eight years.

George Halas—Papa Bear was a standout end and member of the All-Pro squad of the 1920s while coaching championship teams.

Dan Hampton—"Danimal" is in the Hall of Fame thanks to a dozen great years (1979–1990) at end and tackle for the Bears, four of which put him in the Pro Bowl.

Bill Hewitt—Non-helmet-wearing Hall of Fame end, was so quick off the snap he appeared to be offside; member of All-Pro squad of the 1930s.

Link Lyman—Also a great offensive player, a tackle who pioneered stunting en route to a Hall of Fame career in the 1920s and 1930s.

Joe Stydahar—Spurned helmets; best known for his defensive prowess at tackle, though he played offense as well; is in Hall of Fame and on All-Pro squad of the 1930s.

George Trafton—Was as mean and tough on defense as he was on offense, where he played a roving—sideline-to-sideline—style in the 1920s.

The season ended swiftly as Tom Landry's powerful Dallas Cowboys demolished the Bears 37–7 in the opening round of the playoffs, en route to winning Super Bowl XII. It hardly mattered to Bears fans, however. Their beloved Bruins had reasons for hope that success would return to the Windy City's lone NFL franchise.

TRIVIA

Which former Vikings defensive player did Jim Finks acquire on October 12, 1978?

Answers to the trivia questions are on pages 182–183.

The team was hardly dominant. Despite their 9–5 record, the Bears scored only two points more than they permitted (255–253). No mention of 1977 is complete without a salute to "Sweetness," however. Payton tore through defenses to the tune of 1,852 yards on 339 carries, for a whopping 5.5 yards per attempt and 14 touchdowns. It was his rushing dominance—more than 24 rushes per game—that absolutely drove the offense.

The New Year opened with a stunner. Jack Pardee announced he was leaving the Bears to take over as head coach in Washington, a more prestigious post given the recent success of George Allen in the nation's capital and his over-the-hill gang, a squad of which Pardee was a prominent member through the 1972 season. Finks went back to his football roots. He looked toward Minnesota and plucked Vikings assistant Neill Armstrong to become the Bears' new head coach.

Armstrong could not have begun more auspiciously. He won his first three games, and the city was buzzing with excitement. Then Chicago lost eight straight games, only to come back to win four of their remaining five. The final number was seven wins and nine losses. In most disappointment would have reigned, but fans would have comforted themselves knowing the team had no real shot at the playoffs. No such comfort was afforded Bears fans in 1978, as the division was taken by the Minnesota Vikings with an 8–7–1 record. Just two more wins anywhere in that eight-game skid and the Bears would have been alive for a run at the Super Bowl. The difference between the 1977 and 1978 editions of the Chicago Bears may have been substantial in the won-lost column, but not in point differential. Whereas the '77 team was but two points superior to its opposition over the 14-game run, the '79 team was just 21 points short (253–274) in 16 games. In 1978 the close ones got away.

TRIVIA

Who was the coach of the Eagles in the 1979 playoff game with the Bears?

Answers to the trivia questions are on pages 182–183.

It was, "Which way Chicago?" in 1979. Would the Bears return to their winning form of 1977, or was the absence of Pardee too much to overcome and Neill Armstrong simply not ready for prime coaching time?

As was the case in '78, the Bears started quickly, taking their first two games. Regrettably, they continued replicating the previous season by dropping five of the next six, leaving them at 3–5 in midseason for the second consecutive year. This time they rebounded in time, however, winning six of their next seven games and heading into the final weekend with a 9–6 record, tied with Tampa Bay in the division. Even a must-win the following week against St. Louis would guarantee nothing. If Tampa Bay beat Kansas City, because the Buccaneers held the tie-breaker edge, the Bears' only hope would be a wild-card ticket, but to get that Dallas would have to defeat Washington and the combined scoring margins would have to reach at least 35 points. The odds were long, but the Bears did their job, capping off the campaign with a 42–6 blowout of the St. Louis Cardinals, aided by some aggressive playing, especially on special teams.

The 36-point margin meant that all that was left was for Dallas to prevail against Washington and the Bears would go into the postseason as a wild-card. The Bears gathered together in the parking lot to listen to the game. "We also needed Dallas to beat Washington," Buffone recalls. "But it looked like Washington was going to win [they were up 17–0 leading in the second quarter]. All of a sudden Staubach, Roger the Dodger, brings the Cowboys back and finally we hear, 'Touchdown!' Dallas won, and we were screaming, 'We're in the playoffs!'" With the Cowboys winning 35–34, the Bears would face the 11–5 Eagles in the playoffs at Philadelphia the following week.

The Eagles struck first on a 17-yard pass from Ron Jaworski to ace wideout Harold Carmichael, but Payton countered with a two-yard run to tie the game. A Tony Franklin field goal gave the Eagles a 10–7 lead until Payton powered over again, this time from the 1, and Thomas kicked a 30-yard field goal to lift the Bears to a 17–10 halftime edge in Philly. That was it, as the Eagles put up 17 unanswered second-half points to win, 27–17.

Again, it hardly mattered. In a decade of painful, forgettable seasons, the Bears had posted two winners in the last three years, washing away some of the ugly memories and feeding Bears fans with the bread of hope.

Indeed it had been a painful 10 years, as Chicago turned in easily its worst decade on the gridiron, going just 60–83–1. It was the first losing decade in the proud history of the franchise. The '80s had better be better if the 84-year-old Halas was to find any joy in football. And joy is what he needed, as team president—and far more important, his only son—54-year-old George "Muggs" Halas Jr., died suddenly of a heart attack on the very day his beloved Bears won their way into the playoffs with the victory over St. Louis.

A Turn in the Road

Two postseason runs in three years had Bears fans waiting for autumn of 1980 with great anticipation. The season opened in Green Bay, and the game turned into a typical Bears-Packers blood struggle. As the clock wound down on the 6–6 tie, the Packers got into position for an easy Chester Marcol game-winning field goal with 10 seconds left. Amazingly, his kick was low, and the Bears' Alan Page stuffed it. Even more amazingly, the ball hopped directly to Marcol, who ran into the end zone with the winner. A 22–3 win the following week over New Orleans was followed by losses to Minnesota and Pittsburgh, and suddenly the Bears were just one up and three down at the season's quarter turn. Almost as bad, the team merely split their next four contests, and at the halfway point Chicago was a behind-the-eight-ball 3–5 and in search of a quarterback among Vince Evans, Mike Phipps, and Bob Avellini.

When the team lost at Cleveland 27–21 the following week the picture looked nearly hopeless. A 4–3 finish gave the team a sorry 7–9 record for what was expected to be a glorious 1980.

A bright spot during the disappointing 1980 season was a late-season 61–7 obliteration of the Green Bay Packers in Soldier Field. Given the razor-thin Green Bay victory in the opener on the Marcol fiasco, the margin of the late-season win defied explanation. It was widely believed, however, that the Bears were stealing the Packers' offensive signals from the sidelines. The charge was never denied.

After a year down, a year up, and then a year down, 1981 was a put-up or shut-up year for Neill Armstrong and his Bears.

They didn't put up at the outset of the season, dropping their first two games to Green Bay at home and San Francisco on the road. A glimmer of hope emerged with a 28–17 win over Tampa Bay, but a losing streak—typical of Armstrong's tenure—of four games buried the Bruins with a 1–6 start. Another three-game losing skid followed, and only a three-game stretch run gave the team six wins in 16 outings.

If Jim Finks was known for anything it was his capacity to make careful though occasionally controversial decisions and then stay the course. Tired of the lack of discipline the quarterback controversies, and absence of team unity, Halas did not want to stay the course. He decided there needed to be a turn in the road. With that Halas overrode Finks by firing the mild-mannered Armstrong, and Finks didn't like it. Halas then, after conferring with the inimitable Tom Landry, hired Mike Ditka from the Cowboys staff as his new head coach. Not surprisingly, Finks resigned in '82 in part because Halas did not consult him in the hiring of Ditka. Finks would join the Cubs front office shortly after.

Ditka's hiring was not without substantial controversy. Many felt the 87-year-old Halas was losing his grip by hiring the former Bear. Ditka was widely regarded as a loose cannon, and despite being on Landry's staff since 1973, had never served as a coordinator on offense or defense. As such, he was viewed as lacking in the X's and O's dimension of the game and likely far too emotional to handle the stress of a head coaching post in the NFL with any equanimity. Having Landry's support, however, was a major plus for Ditka, as Halas sounded out the great Cowboys mentor at length about his coaching potential.

Chicago fans were divided on the choice. On one hand, they wanted more fire than they saw in Armstrong, and the return of one of the family to run the team sat well with many of them. On the other, there was concern that Ditka was all glands and lacking in the kind of sound football acumen now so highly prized in NFL coaches.

Mike Ditka was eager and excited. He made no apology for his passion for the game or intent to restore the Bears to prominence. Taking over his favorite team was simply a dream come true. Moreover, the apprenticeship under Landry in addition to the retention of Defensive Coordinator Buddy Ryan figured to serve him well in the deeper aspects of the game.

No one was terribly sure about what to expect from Ditka and the

TRIVIA

Who held the career rushing record before Payton?

Answers to the trivia questions are on pages 182–183.

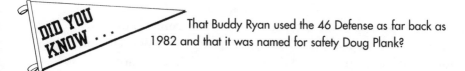

That Buddy Ryan used the 46 Defense as far back as 1982 and that it was named for safety Doug Plank?

Bears in 1982, other than that it would be entertaining. Early on, the new coach emphasized his lack of tolerance for anything other than all-out hustle and commitment. He held a minicamp in May in which there was simply ferocious hitting in the most demanding of atmospheres. The new coach made it clear that the aim was the Super Bowl and only players willing to pay the price would be kept around to enjoy the success. Regrettably, he did not have enough quality horses in the 1982 stable, and the team went just 3–6–0 in his strike-shortened inaugural year. With Vince Evans and Bob Avellini slated to see action at quarterback, Ditka's Bears, soon to be quarterbacked by rookie Jim McMahon who had had a storied career at Brigham Young, ranked 22nd among the 28 teams in points scored, with 141.

Of consolation to Chicago fans, however, was that the new coach did not seem in over his head, most certainly did not lack confidence, and seemed absolutely driven to turn the Bears into champions. There was nothing listless, diffident, or foggy about Ditka. He was candid, unbending, and driven.

Ditka wanted it turned around in 1983. McMahon was in his second year, Payton was at his peak, Dan Hampton and Mike Singletary were stars, and the draft had been rich. Jimbo Covert, Willie Gault, Mike Richardson, Dave Duerson, Tom Thayer, Richard Dent, and Mark Bortz were all drafted in 1983.

A grinding 20–17 loss to Atlanta chilled the opening of the season, but the team came back with a 17–10 home win over Tampa Bay. The season might have looked very different had the Bears not lost two consecutive overtime decisions to New Orleans and Baltimore to drop to 1–3. They went on to split the next four, putting them at an unimpressive 3–5 at the halfway point. They fell to 3–6 (the same record as 1982) the following week with an embarrassing 38–17 spanking from the Lions in Chicago.

If that were not disappointing enough, the very next day, October 31, 1983, George Stanley Halas died of pancreatic cancer. He was 88 years old.

Despite the Bears' sorry start under Ditka, Halas believed in his young, 44-year-old coach. Just prior to his passing, Halas gave Ditka a present, but told him not to open it until after the team won the Super Bowl. The emotional mentor vowed he would make that happen.

The loss of Halas seemed to congeal the team. After losing to the Rams 21–14 in Los Angeles, Chicago raced down the stretch, winning five of their remaining six to close the 1983 books at 8–8. The season was a disappointment to Ditka, but the team was young, it was finally winning, and Bears fans could feel their coach was relentless in finishing the task of getting to the Super Bowl.

The future was now, as far as the coach was concerned, and his charges blew out of the gate in 1984 with three straight wins. With McMahon out with an injury in the third game—a frequent theme in the quarterback's Chicago career—Ditka turned to Bob Avellini as his field

Dallas Cowboys head coach Tom Landry's strong endorsement of Mike Ditka, here together on the sideline with Roger Staubach during the 1972 Super Bowl, was instrumental in Ditka's hiring as the Bears head coach.

general. The team scored just nine points against Forrest Gregg's Packers, but it was enough to win, 9–7. They scored only nine again the following week in a 38–9 pummeling by Seattle, and the decisive Ditka cut Avellini. A 23–14 loss to Dallas followed, and the team was just 3–2.

A major story was developing during 1984, and it figured to hit in Game 6 against the Saints. The incomparable Walter Payton was poised to break the NFL career rushing mark in this, his 10th season. The record came in the third quarter of a 20–7 home win. After two wins in its next three games the Bears had a 6–3 record and a date with the NFL champion Raiders in Soldier Field the following week. After McMahon was flattened with a lacerated kidney, putting him out for the season, the Bears defense, led by Richard Dent with three sacks, tore into Raiders quarterback Marc Wilson en route to a 17–6 win.

With journeyman quarterback Steve Fuller at the throttle, the team followed a loss to the Rams in Los Angeles with a pair of wins, and the 9–4 Chicago Bears were the NFC Central Division champions.

Adversity struck again, however, as Fuller was injured and the team turned to an inexperienced Rusty Lisch in the next game at San Diego. The team lost 20–7 and followed that with another sputtering effort against the Pack, one in which none other than Walter Payton lined up in the shotgun after Lisch was unable to generate sufficient offense in what turned out to be a 20–14 loss. The Bears then acquired 14-year veteran signal caller Greg Landry to start the finale at Detroit, and he contributed to a 30–13 win.

The good news was that Steve Fuller would be back for the playoffs. The bad news was that the opening game was at Washington against the 1983 NFC champions. The underdog Bears, on the strength of scoring passes by Fuller and Payton—on the running back option—escaped from the East Coast with a stunning 23–19 win.

A week later they would go west to San Francisco to play for the NFC championship. Bill Walsh's 49ers keyed on Payton, and Fuller was unable to penetrate the strong San Francisco secondary as the 49ers sent the Bears home with a 23–0 defeat.

So they had come up short, but really, so what? The Bears were growling again, Ditka was the tough guy the franchise needed to bring back the fire of the departed Papa Bear—George Halas—the team was maturing into a power, and 1985 looked very promising.

All-Time Bears

Defensive Backs (listed alphabetically)

J. C. Caroline—Was part of a solid defensive corps of the 1950s and 1960s and was picked to the Pro Bowl in his rookie season.

Mark Carrier—Played three times in the Pro Bowl during his seven years with the Bears, beginning in 1990; was a standout during difficult seasons.

Dave Duerson—Played with powerful Bears teams from 1983 to 1989 and was on four Pro Bowl squads.

Gary Fencik—Twelve-year Bear, beginning in 1976, was All-Pro and Pro Bowl pick as leader in the Chicago secondary.

Shaun Gayle—Played on eight Bears playoff teams, from 1984 to 1994, and was Pro Bowl pick in 1991.

Red Grange—Great as he was on offensive in his heyday, the Hall of Fame "Galloping Ghost" was better known for his great play in the defensive backfield.

George McAfee—Hall of Fame star through the 1940s and member of All-Pro squad of that decade; picked off 25 enemy aerials.

Richie Petitbon—Played a decade for the Bears (1959–1968) and was on the Pro Bowl team four of those seasons.

Roosevelt Taylor—Star of the 1960s, Taylor was All-Pro in the championship 1963 season and a two-time Pro Bowl honoree.

Donnell Woolford—Third all-time in interceptions, was Pro Bowl pick in his fifth season (1993) of eight-year Bears career.

The Year That Was

The 1985 Chicago Bears' season is very nearly impossible to capture in words. It was one of those near mythical times, one in which a buzz was forever in the air and the Bears were on every Chicago fan's mind. After the sudden turnaround from a 3–6 record in 1982 to an 8–8 in '83 and then a 10–6 push in 1984, Chicago fans placed full confidence in Ditka and what was now a truly impressive array of football talent wearing the blue and orange.

Fans could hardly wait for the team to get the preseason over with and start pursuing a Super Bowl appearance. The regular season opened at home against the Buccaneers, and it did not open well. Tampa Bay held a halftime edge, and the fans were getting restless. In the second half, however, the Chicago offense stirred and the game went into the Bears' win column by a 38–28 margin. In Game 2, it was Buddy Ryan's 46 Defense as the Patriots fell 20–7. The fast start was in jeopardy the following Thursday evening when the Vikings held a 17–9 lead in the third quarter. McMahon, sidelined by a neck injury, watched as Fuller could not move the team. He then began lobbying Ditka for an opportunity to get into the action and try to salvage the game. Ditka caved, and McMahon threw three TD passes in a 33–24 win. A win like that had many fans feeling there might be something very special about 1985.

The Bears took it to Washington to the tune of 45–10, then followed that with two road wins—a 27–19 conquest of Tampa Bay and a 26–10 win against the 49ers. The San Francisco game was huge, as it was a rematch between the 1984 NFC championship combatants. Ditka remembered well the 49ers mentor's late-game insertion of offensive lineman Guy McIntyre into the San Francisco backfield to drive home

Jim McMahon dives over for a touchdown in Super Bowl XX against the New England Patriots, a game the Bears dominated.

By the NUMBERS

1985 Bears vs. 1972 Dolphins

The only NFL champion to go undefeated during the regular season was the 1972 Miami Dolphins. A quick comparison looks like this.

	PPG Avg.	Rank	PG Allowed	Rank	Margin	Rank
Miami	27.5	1	12.2	1	15.3	1
Chicago	28.5	2	12.4	1	16.1	1

another 49ers score. He sent Walsh a message in the form of 300-plus-pound rookie defensive lineman William "The Refrigerator" Perry from Clemson, and an icon was born.

By then the entire football nation was taking note of Ditka's modern-day Monsters of the Midway. Although the Packers hardly figured to be in the Bears' class, they were the Packers, and they were next at Soldier Field. They left as 23–7 *Monday Night Football* losers, having been treated to Perry's blocking and his snowplow-like touchdown. Six days later the Bears finished the first half of the season at a perfect 8–0 with a 27–9 win over the Vikings in Chicago.

Forrest Gregg's Packers were not happy about the *Monday Night* humiliation and the antics of The Refrigerator. They brought their defensive A-game out in a vicious struggle on Wisconsin turf, but Chicago prevailed by a lean 16–10 count, with Perry collecting a touchdown aerial in the first half.

Clearly the Bears were more than good. They were perhaps great, and they showed it with a 24–3 win over Detroit, an inexplicable 44–0 drubbing of the Cowboys in Dallas—one about which Ditka did not feel elated, given his admiration and affection for Cowboys coach Tom Landry—and a 36–0 hammering of Atlanta. The 46 Defense was awesome, having yielded only 29 points in the previous six games.

At 12–0, the team prepared for another *Monday Night Football* date, this time against the Dolphins in Miami. The 8–4 Dolphins had been a Super Bowl team a year ago, falling to the 49ers. They were led by Don Shula and a young second-year quarterback named Dan Marino. It was all Miami in this one, as the Bears suffered their first loss, 38–24. The Dolphins would sweep their next three to finish 12–4.

Chicago beat a rather weak (5–11 on the season) Indianapolis team the following week by an unimpressive 17–10 score. A 19–6 road win against the tough Jets gave the team a 14–1 mark with only one regular-season date left, at Detroit against the struggling Lions. A 37–17 pounding of the Lions closed perhaps the most dominating season in Bears football lore. The team scored 456 points, second-best in the league, and permitted a puny 198, best among the 28 NFL teams. Their net point margin was a whopping 258—an average of better than 16 points per game. In looking back on the season, Ditka thought:

> We won most of the early games with offense; our defense was kind of not sure yet. They were still getting their feet wet, and everybody had kind of picked on that defense. Other teams knew when we were blitzing and this and that, but then once the defense cranked it up it didn't matter if they knew or not, because nobody could stop them. As the season went along, our cornerbacks got more confidence, our people covered receivers like blankets—they had a lot of confidence. By the end of the year you could see from other teams playing us that they didn't want any part of those guys, nor our defensive line or linebackers. Those guys were just awfully good. And they were brutal.

Despite the near all-conquering nature of the '85 team, Bears fans were braced for less than the full measure of success, a Super Bowl championship, given the sports curse that apparently hung over the Windy City. In 1969 all looked so promising for Leo Durocher's Cubs, who only broke the hearts of Cubs fans worldwide with a September melt-down. In 1983 the White Sox looked to many to be World Series timber, only to have La Russa's Sox disappear unceremoniously to the Baltimore Orioles in the ALCS. The very next year it was the Cubs again. They not only roared to a divisional championship, but they also led two games to

That ESPN selected the 1985 Chicago Bears as the greatest team in the history of the NFL?

TRIVIA

What rather presumptuous thing did the Bears do the day after their loss to the Dolphins that caused permanent memories but some consternation among Bears officials?

Answers to the trivia questions are on pages 182–183.

none in a best-of-five NLCS vs. the San Diego Padres. Then, of course, the unimaginable happened. The baby bears were swept, and all the fans had were the shards of their broken hearts.

So against the backdrop of such memories the Bears opened the play-offs at home against the Giants. Rather than choke, the team was simply dominant, hanging a 21–0 whitewash on the New Yorkers. Now it was back to the NFC title game, this time against John Robinson's Los Angeles Rams. Same result—the Bears pounded the Rams 24–0 in Soldier Field—and believe it or not, the Chicago Bears, coached by Michael Keller Ditka, would represent the NFC in Super Bowl XX to be played in New Orleans.

In the Super Bowl the Bears finished off the 1985 championship season with an exclamation point, burying the New England Patriots, 46–10, the biggest blowout in Super Bowl history up to that time. Bears owner Mike McCaskey recalls fondly, "You could just feel the exuberance and excitement that were coursing through the Bears team that year. The fans picked up the momentum and the rich enjoyment of it all." After the Patriots scored first in the Super Bowl and the scoreboard flashed the news that in the preceding 19 Super Bowls the team that scored first had won 17 of them, McCaskey recalled, "But then, of course, everything changed. Our offense exploded. The defense was impenetrable. We were like a huge boa constrictor just squeezing down and squeezing down; there was no question we were going to win this game. It was such a thrill, I didn't want to ever see it end."

But it was over. The Bears had given Chicago sports fans everything they could have possibly wanted, and Mike Ditka had fulfilled his promise to the departed George Halas. All that was left was the establishment of a dynasty.

'85 Bears by the Roster and Numbers

Perhaps the greatest team in Bears history, maybe even NFL history, was assembled primarily through the draft. The following is a list of the key performers from the 1985 Bears, including some thoughts on the season from a handful of them.

Offense

QB Jim McMahon—The Brigham Young star ran the offense, throwing for 15 TDs and injecting confidence in the previously maligned offense. "I think the third game, that Thursday night up in Minnesota, was the milestone of the season. I think we knew after that we were on our way and nobody was going to stop us. We showed we could turn it around if we had to. ... On the plane up to Minneapolis, Ditka came over and told me I wasn't going to play [due to a leg infection]. ... The first half didn't go all that well, and the start of the second wasn't any better. We were losing 17–9. So I was in Ditka's ear most of the time on the sideline about putting me in. Steve [Fuller] wasn't playing all that bad; it's just that the team wasn't getting anything done. We needed a spark, change. Finally, Ditka looked over at me and said, 'Get your [butt] in there and throw a screen pass.' So, I called a screen pass. But as I was dropping back I stumbled. They were blitzing, and I saw the linebackers coming as I was regaining my balance. What I also saw suddenly was Willie Gault running free down the middle, so I just unloaded to him, and it was a 70-yard touchdown."

LT Jim Covert—the Pro Bowl player out of Pittsburgh was anchor on the offensive line.

LG Mark Bortz—At the zenith of his career the former Hawkeye received a game ball for his punishing blocking early in the season vs. Washington.

C Jay Hilgenberg—Another Hawkeye in his fifth year at center for the Bears. He and his fellow Iowa star would be mainstays on the powerful Bears line for years to come.

RG Tom Thayer—Played all 16 games as a rookie and became an NFL star as an offensive lineman.

RT Keith Van Horne—Beginning in 1981 out of USC, Van Horne lasted 13 years as a Bears lineman.

TE Emery Moorehead—Acquired from Denver prior to the 1981 season, Moorehead caught 200 passes over eight seasons for the Bears as a tough blocking tight end.

WR Willie Gault—With just blazing speed, Gault gave the Bears their much-needed deep threat, averaging 21.3 yards per catch in 1985.

WR Dennis McKinnon—Caught seven TD passes to lead the '85 team; caught a pair of scores in the big second-half comeback early in the season in Minnesota.

RB Walter Payton—Arguably the greatest football player of all time. Gained more than 1,500 yards in his 11th season with the team. Was league MVP in 1985.

FB Matt Suhey—Outstanding blocking back for Payton, this Penn State star ran for 471 yards as Walter's running mate.

Defense

RE Richard Dent—Led team in sacks; was Super Bowl XX MVP, forcing two fumbles: Dent was one of the truly great NFL pass rushers.

RT William Perry—The first-round pick for the Bears in the '85 draft, The Fridge became a cult hero for his defensive line play, his rushing, and even his pass receiving.

LT Steve McMichael—Received All-NFL acclaim in 1985 and was a Pro Bowl selection on more than one occasion. Out of Texas, McMichael played 13 of his 15 NFL seasons with the Bears.

LE Dan Hampton—Hall of Fame star for Chicago, Danimal could play tackle or end. A six-time All-NFL performer, he played for the Bears in three different decades. "The players as a whole were really committed to the fact that this was going to be our year. We were not going to let it go without a fight. A lot of teams tried their damnedest to beat us that year—they'd give us their best shot—and we just rocked them week after week, except for that awful game down in Miami."

OLB Otis Wilson—A Pro Bowl selection in 1985, Wilson joined the Bears in 1980 out of Louisville. His tough demeanor earned him the nickname The Junkyard Dog.

MLB Mike Singletary—The premier middle linebacker of his time, Singletary entered the Hall of Fame in 1998. As fine a Christian as one

William Perry, "The Fridge," here spiking the ball after scoring a touchdown in Super Bowl XX, was the embodiment of the 1985 Bears, a team of colorful personalities that kicked your butt in ruthless fashion on the field.

That though long gone from the Bears by 1985, Jim Finks drafted 19 of the 22 Super Bowl XX Chicago starters?

could find off the field, the hard-tackling Singletary was the brains of the defense on the gridiron. All-NFC nine times, he played in 10 consecutive Pro Bowls. "It went by too fast that year. It just flew by. I hardly got to taste it. It seemed like so much was happening. Every time you turned your head it was something new. Somebody was doing another commercial. Somebody was doing another shoot. It was an exciting year. There was just so much going on. And the 'Super Bowl Shuffle.' I thought it was one of the dumbest things I'd ever done in my life. But, you know, I still appreciate ... why we did it. I was reluctant at first, but Willie Gault told me that the money was going to the needy, and on that basis, I did it."

OLB Wilber Marshall—In his first season as a full-time starter, the Florida star was—according to Ditka—the best outside linebacker in football when he played for the Bears.

SS Dave Duerson—Duerson was a four-time Pro Bowl pick. The 1985 season was Duerson's first as a starter. He led NFL strong safeties with five interceptions.

FS Gary Fencik—The Yale veteran Fencik had been with Chicago since 1976. Still a solid player, Fencik played through 1987, making two Pro Bowl teams. "The week before the Super Bowl down there in New Orleans was great fun. It was a work week for us, but Ditka let us party, and there was no curfew. I think everyone was pretty relaxed. We never even saw any of the Patriots. They were under a very strict regimen. I think Ditka pretty much knew his team, knew that we were really going for it. We had confidence because of our season and two playoff games, and we had beaten the Patriots earlier that year [20–7]."

LCB Leslie Frazier—Frazier blew out his knee early in the Super Bowl, ending his career in his fifth season, just as he was about to reach for greatness. A man of great faith, Frazier regathered himself and at 28 was head coach at Trinity, a Christian college in Deerfield, Illinois.

RCB Mike Richardson—From Arizona State, Richardson played six of his seven years for the Bears. He was a third-year man when he picked off four passes for the Super Bowl Bears.

Other Notables

PK Kevin Butler—Butler was a real coup, a fourth-round pick out of Georgia. He hit on all his PATs and more than 80 percent of his field-goal attempts and tallied 144 points.

TRIVIA

LB Jim Morrissey—Although not heavily used in 1985 owing to the dominance of the team's linebacking corps, this 11th-round pick from Michigan State became a stellar performer for Chicago in years to come.

P Maury Buford—Picked up from San Diego in the off-season, Buford not only averaged better than 42 yards per punt, but he also placed 18 inside the opponents' 20.

LB Ron Rivera—Rivera was a sound contributor from the bench on defense and excelled on special teams. As in the case of Morrissey, he became a solid linebacker in future seasons.

OG Kurt Becker—Becker was actually the starting right guard for the first four contests, before he went down with an injury.

QB Steve Fuller—Backing up the oft-injured McMahon, Fuller started five games under center.

WR Dennis Gentry—Gentry was an all-purpose performer, particularly adept at returning kicks and pass receiving. He had game-breaking ability.

DE Mike Hartenstine—Hartenstine was the starting left defensive end for the first seven games. Dan Hampton took his place, moving over from defensive tackle when The Fridge was ready to start in the interior defensive line.

1985 by the Numbers

	Rsh. Ydg.	Rank	P. Ydg.	Rank	TY	Rank
Team Offense	2,761	1	3,303	22	6,064	6
Team Defense	1,319	1	3,299	6	4,618	1

Rushing

	Att.	Ydg.	Avg.	TDs
Walter Payton	324	1,551	4.8	9
Matt Suhey	115	471	4.1	1

Passing

	Att.	Com.	Pct.	Ydg.	Avg.	TD	Int.	Rating
Jim McMahon	313	178	56.9	2,392	7.64	15	11	82.6
Steve Fuller	107	53	49.5	777	7.26	1	5	57.3

Receiving

	No.	Ydg.	Avg.	TDs
Walter Payton	49	483	9.9	2
Emery Moorehead	35	481	13.7	1
Willie Gault	33	704	21.3	1
Matt Suhey	33	295	8.9	1
Dennis McKinnon	31	555	17.9	7
Tim Wrightman	24	407	17.0	1

Kickoff Returns

	No.	Ydg.	Avg.	TDs
Willie Gault	22	577	26.2	1
Dennis Gentry	18	466	25.9	1

Punt Returns

	No.	Ydg.	Avg.	TDs
Ken Taylor	25	198	7.9	0
Keith Ortego	7	158	9.3	0

Punting

	No.	Ydg.	Avg.
Maury Buford	68	2,870	42.2

Place-Kicking

	PAT Att.	PAT	Fga.	Fg.	Pct.	Points
Kevin Butler	51	51	37	31	83.8	144

Interceptions

	No.	Yd. Ret.	Avg.	TDs
Leslie Frazier	6	119	19.8	1
Dave Duerson	5	53	10.6	0
Gary Fencik	5	43	8.6	0
Mike Richardson	4	174	43.5	1

Sacks

	No.
Richard Dent	17.0
Otis Wilson	10.5
Steve McMichael	8.0
Dan Hampton	6.5
Wilber Marshall	6.0
William Perry	5.0

Da Bears

Coming off 1985—and four straight years of improvement under Mike Ditka, whose NFL coaching record was now 36–21 (and 4–1 in the post-season)—Bear fans were expecting the team to go from strength to strength, dominating the NFL as Lombardi's Packers had two decades previous.

Their expectations were dealt a substantial jolt when, early in 1986, Defensive Coordinator Buddy Ryan's feud with Ditka went public and he accepted the job as head coach of the Philadelphia Eagles. The simmering rift had a lengthy history. Ryan had taken over as defensive coordinator in 1978 under Neill Armstrong. When Armstrong was dismissed, a number of people in the Bears organization—and not the least of whom, Ryan—wanted Buddy as the new head mentor. If nothing else, Ryan tended to have excellent relations with his players. Moreover, his 46 Defense—a system that put all-out pressure on the quarterback, racking up sacks before the besieged signal caller could throw the ball away—was immensely popular with the players and fans. Veteran Alan Page wrote Halas a letter, beseeching him to keep Ryan, a letter signed by all of the team's defensive players. Halas retained Ryan, signing him to a multiyear deal prior to hiring Ditka as the main man.

From there the tension simply escalated between the two high-profile, power-seeking personalities. Ryan, for his part, piled up credentials, fashioning his 46 Defense into an exciting attacking bunch that contributed substantially to the team's scoring numbers by forcing turnovers and establishing desirable field position. To Ditka's credit, he gave Ryan a wide berth with the defense, permitting the crusty coordinator almost exclusive run of that side of the team. On one occasion

Ditka intruded in a defensive meeting only to be told by Ryan to get out and leave "his" players alone.

Things boiled over between the two during the lone loss of 1985, against the Dolphins, when Ryan refused to put in a secondary man to cover Nat Moore, Miami's fleet wide receiver, instead of linebacker Wilber Marshall. The rebuffed Ditka told Ryan that the coordinator had the choice of getting his behind whipped physically or deferring to his leadership. Although little is known of what happened after the exchange, the air got only cooler between the two, and when the final gun sounded after the Super Bowl win, Ryan was carried off by a number of his defensive players while Ditka was hoisted to the shoulders of other Bears.

TRIVIA

What is Buddy Ryan's real first name?

Answers to the trivia questions are on pages 182–183.

The fissure could hardly have been more graphic, and Ditka went public with it. After the truculent Ryan left for Philly, Ditka installed the more temperate Vince Tobin in the defensive coordinator's role. While Tobin did not employ the attacking style of Ryan, the team's defense continued to excel. Ryan managed to shape the Eagles into a defensively oriented contender in the NFC East, although never able to make a big playoff run.

So by 1986 Mike Ditka was the man and Da Bears continued to win. The year began with the coach unhappy with the bloated condition of then 220-pound Jim McMahon. On the plus side, however, the organization—with Payton then 32, albeit still going strong—nabbed running back Neal Anderson from Florida with its first choice. The Bears took out Cleveland 41–31 in the opener and followed that with an emotional 13–10 win over Buddy Ryan's new team. Four straight wins followed in which the Bears yielded only 26 points, and the team was well on its way to a big '86 with a 6–0 mark. Defeat was tasted in the Hubert H. Humphrey Metrodome, however, as the Vikings disposed of the Bruins 23–7. McMahon suffered yet another injury, and Steve Fuller took over with little success. A 13–7 win over Detroit was followed by a 20–17 home loss to the Los Angeles Rams.

That, however, was the end of the losing, as the team won its last seven in a row, never yielding more than 14 points in any of the games.

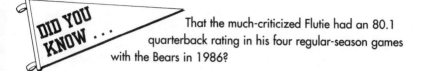

That the much-criticized Flutie had an 80.1 quarterback rating in his four regular-season games with the Bears in 1986?

The final record read 14 wins and just two losses. Moreover, Buddy was all but forgotten as the Tobin-led defense helped hold the opposition to just 187 points, 11 fewer than in 1985. The offense, however, was not the same, tallying just 352 points compared to 456 in '85.

A major subplot of 1986 was the signing of Doug Flutie. With McMahon frequently injured, Fuller not effective, and Mike Tomczak not ready, the acquisition made sense. Flutie, however, was not well received by the quarterback corps, and another split developed, as the 5'8" former Heisman Trophy winner played increasingly more minutes.

They faced a 12–4 Washington squad in the divisional playoffs. Unfortunately, the overwhelmingly favored Bears did not give any indication that the assignment was easy, as they fell by a 27–13 score in Soldier Field. The season was over, and the fans were understandably stunned. That the team was quarterbacked by Flutie did nothing for Ditka, Flutie, or club unity. He was gone to New England by 1987.

With fans hoping the early playoff exit in '86 was but a blip on the Bears' radar screen of success, the 1987 season opened with Ditka and McMahon at odds in part because the team had the temerity to draft a quarterback, Jim Harbaugh of Michigan, at No. 1. Furthermore, on the larger NFL front, labor tensions dominated the early season, resulting in a work stoppage after the second game—a point at which Chicago was 2–0 and led in part by Tomczak, as McMahon and Fuller were injured and Harbaugh was too green.

Ditka lined up on the side of management when the work stoppage hit, and—after an idle week due to the strike—managed to go 2–1 with a squad of replacement players that Ditka called the "real Bears," not exactly endearing him to his players. When the strike ended and the regulars returned, McMahon was back at quarterback, and the team reeled off three straight wins, including a 27–26 win over Tampa Bay in a contest in which the Bears trailed 20–0. The third

TRIVIA

What season-turning event occurred in Game 12 of 1986 in Green Bay?

Answers to the trivia questions are on pages 182–183.

was a heart-thumping 26–24 win at Lambeau over the Pack on a 52-yard field goal by Kevin Butler. A loss to Denver followed, but the team rallied and won the next two. At 10–2, Chicago inexplicably lost a pair of games, including a 41–0 drubbing in San Francisco, before edging the Los Angeles Raiders 6–3 in the finale to finish at 11–4 in a 15-game season. For the shortened season the team put up 356 points, four more than in the 16-game '86 campaign, but permitted 282, fully 95 more points than the previous season in one fewer game.

There was plenty of incentive for the Bears to get out of the playoff gate quickly after the '87 season, as the team drew a rematch with an 11–4 Washington bunch, again in Soldier Field. But the team fell once again, this time 21–17, in a game in which the incomparable Payton—now in his final year—barely missed a first down during the team's final drive, ending his career with a bitter taste.

Jim McMahon, here working the crowd during Super Bowl XX, was rebellious and untamed, a style that rarely served him well on the field.

Sweetness

"Sweetness"—it was the perfect nickname for Walter Payton, a man who left an indelible mark on football and life during his 45 earthly years. He was sweet to watch, sweet to coach, sweet to the fans, and sweet in disposition. He was also a great, great player. He was easily the greatest Bear of all time, greater than Nagurski, Luckman, Butkus, and Sayers. But it is larger than that. "I thought Walter Payton was the greatest football player who ever lived," said commentator John Madden, putting it succinctly.

Born on July 25, 1954, in Columbia, Mississippi, Payton's star rose swiftly, and seemingly out of nowhere. Payton did not spend his college years at a highly publicized major college football power. He was a two-time Little All-American at Jackson State, good enough to be the No. 1 Chicago Bears draft choice in 1975.

He ran for 679 yards in his rookie year and (other than in strike-shortened 1982) never again ran for less than 1,200 yards in a single season until his final year 12 seasons later. When he was finished he had gained 16,726 yards on the ground—by far the highest total in NFL history as of his retirement. He was either first or second in in NFL rushing six times, in the top five on nine occasions. He once gained 275 yards in a single game and rushed for more than 100 yards 77 different times. Moreover, in his rookie year Sweetness won the NFL kickoff-return title. But he did more than run. This nine-time Pro Bowl player also managed to catch nearly 500 NFL passes (492) for another 4,538 yards. Touchdowns? He tallied 110 of them on the ground and 15 more through the air. But he did more than run and catch. He threw eight TD passes. But he did more than run, catch, and throw. He was also among the best blocking backs of his time.

And perhaps most amazing of all, he managed to do all this for an organization that had just two winning seasons in the first nine years of his career. Perhaps even more amazing than that, Payton—at just 5'10", 200 pounds, smaller than most NFL power runners—missed only one game in his entire career.

"I wish there was another word I could think of other than *greatness*," remarked Hall of Fame teammate Mike Singletary of the seven-time All-Pro Payton, who was the NFL MVP in 1977 and 1985. "That's what comes to mind, *greatness*." Quarterback Jim McMahon said Payton "was the strongest man I met in my entire life."

Beyond the dizzying heights of his on-the-field career, Walter Payton was loved. "After Brian Piccolo died, my husband and I promised ourselves

Walter Payton, here celebrating after becoming the all-time rushing leader with 12,317 yards in 1984, was a hard-nosed and hard-driving player who for many Bears fans was the consummate athlete and Chicago Bear.

Walter Payton

	RUSHING				PASS RECEIVING			
Year	Att.	Ydg.	Avg.	TDs	No.	Ydg.	Avg.	TDs
1975	196	679	3.5	7	33	213	6.5	0
1976	311	1,390	4.5	13	15	149	9.9	0
1977	339	1,852	5.5	14	27	269	10.0	2
1978	333	1,395	4.2	11	50	480	9.6	0
1979	369	1,610	4.4	14	31	313	10.1	2
1980	317	1,460	4.6	6	46	367	8.0	1
1981	339	1,222	3.6	6	41	379	9.2	2
1982	148	596	4.0	1	32	311	9.7	0
1983	314	1,421	4.5	6	53	607	11.5	2
1984	381	1,684	4.4	11	45	368	8.2	0
1985	324	1,551	4.8	9	49	483	9.9	2
1986	321	1,333	4.2	8	37	483	9.9	3
1987	146	533	3.7	4	33	217	6.6	1
	3,838	16,726	4.4	110	492	4,538	9.2	15

we wouldn't be so personally involved with the players," recalled Halas's daughter, Virginia McCaskey. "We were able to follow that resolve until Walter Payton came into our lives."

"He was a great guy, a great human being, a very giving person," said the elder Jim Mora. Rather than self-aggrandizing, Payton was philanthropic. He and his wife, Connie, founded the Walter & Connie Payton Foundation dedicated "to the emotional healing of neglected, abused, and underprivileged children by providing tools and opportunities to build self-esteem and encourage a better family unit, giving hope for a brighter future." Beyond the foundation, Payton was involved in countless kindnesses to fans in general and children in particular.

His death chilled a city and a football nation. In February 1999, Payton, obviously ill and shrunken in size, disclosed publicly that he needed a liver transplant. He then all but disappeared from public view, with his fans expecting and praying that they would soon hear that their hero had successfully sustained a liver transplant. Afflicted with cancer of the bile duct, however, his disease escalated so quickly that his physicians soon determined that the transplant was no longer a realistic option. By November 1 of that same year the stunning news hit the airwaves: Walter Payton was dead at 45.

That was it. It was over for Sweetness. It was over for the larger-than-life player and personality, one who loved to be the prankster by occasionally (and of course anonymously) answering the switchboard at Bears headquarters or setting off firecrackers in a rookie's locker. In fact, as he faced the end, he still had the spirit to send teammate Matt Suhey to a series of wrong addresses in Suhey's efforts to find Mike Singletary's home. "It was his duty to bring humor and light in any situation. The Bears had some tough years," said Singletary, "and Walter was always the guy who, no matter how tough it was, would always make you feel great about playing the game and playing for the Bears. As a person, he was a bright spot for any darkness that appeared."

TRIVIA

Against which team did Payton gain 275 rushing yards?
BONUS QUIZ QUESTION:
In which year did he do it?

Answers to the trivia questions are on pages 182–183.

Singletary, who spent a great deal of time with Payton in Walter's final days, testified to Payton's character. "This weekend, having the opportunity to spend as much time with him as I could, reading scriptures with him and praying for him—with him; outside of anything else I've seen, the greatest run, the greatest moves—what I experienced this weekend was by far the best of Walter Payton I've ever seen."

"We knew him as a player, the greatest of all time," said Hall of Fame teammate Dan Hampton. "And we knew him as a man, as good as you will find on this planet."

DID YOU KNOW . . . That despite playing at Jackson State, not a major football school, Payton was fourth in the Heisman Trophy voting in 1974?

The Curious Comedown

By 1988 the look of the Bears had changed. New president Michael McCaskey had fired Ditka crony Jerry Vainisi as general manager, several high-priced players were not retained, and Ditka's grip on the organization was being loosened. The team entered the season without the retired Walter Payton and veteran safety Gary Fencik, who also called it quits. Perhaps worse, Washington made an offer to Wilber Marshall that the Bears declined to match, and wide receiver Willie Gault opted to play in Los Angeles, where he could also pursue an acting career.

While the defense continued to perform wonderfully, the offense was erratic. The immature antics of the often-injured McMahon were wearing the team thin, but none of the backups—Fuller, Flutie, or Tomczak—was able to take hold and drive the offense forward. In short, Bears fans had reason to feel unsettled about 1988. But they needn't have. Ditka's squad broke out of the gate quickly, a trademark of the mentor's style, winning seven of their first eight games. The only loss was a 31–7 home routing by Minnesota in Game 3, after which Ditka, in his typical effort to play mind games to stimulate his players, stated the team would be fortunate to make the playoffs as a wild-card.

The Bears fell to 7–2 when New England, with Flutie throwing a TD bomb for the first score, took down the Bears 30–7 on the road, after which the city was stunned by the news that Ditka had suffered a heart attack. The Bears, with Tobin on the sideline, rebounded with a 28–10 conquest of Tampa Bay, and a more sober, rested, and measured Ditka returned to lead the Bears to a 34–14 win at Washington the following week. A 3–2 finish put the team in the playoffs with an impressive 12–4 record, good enough to assure them a home-field advantage throughout. Neal Anderson ran for 1,106 yards, and the Bears' made-over defense was

DID YOU KNOW . . . That in the 1991 overtime win over the Jets, Cap Boso seemingly scored the winning TD on a pass from Harbaugh? The Bears headed to the showers, but the officials spotted the ball on the one, making the Bears return to the field from their dressing room to resume the game. Harbaugh then sneaked in the winner for a 19–13 victory.

ranked No. two in total yardage and tops in fewest points allowed for the season. Their first opponents would be none other than Buddy Ryan and his refurbished, 10–6 Philadelphia Eagles.

Amid a pea-soup-like fog in Soldier Field, the Bears prevailed 20–12, with Tomczak calling signals. The 49ers, another 10–6 squad, were next. The arctic weather conditions favored the Bears over the West Coast opponents in the NFC championship game, but a question remained. With McMahon now healthy, who would be the quarterback? It didn't matter. Although Ditka tabbed McMahon, the quarterback of the day was Joe Montana, who led the Niners to an easy 28–3 win. It was a disappointing finish to an unexpectedly strong season.

While Ditka was losing control inside the organization, he was establishing himself as a likely Hall of Fame mentor on the field with a 73–31 record going into 1989. He had gone a remarkable 37–10 since his Super Bowl year. The team dealt McMahon to the Chargers before the season opened, causing the departure of Offensive Coordinator Ed Hughes, who took umbrage at the move. QB coach Greg Landry stepped in as coordinator; Tomczak, backed by Harbaugh, was to be the signal caller. The team opened with four straight wins in which it scored 129 points, leaving few concerned about the quarterback situation. Moreover, the fourth win was particularly sweet, a 27–13 hammering of Ryan's Eagles at Soldier Field.

The season-long loss of Hampton after the Eagles game signaled what would be an injury-riddled '89 season for the defense, so much so that only two defenders would start all 16 games. The loss of Hampton was felt as the team embarked on a most uncharacteristic three-game skid. They then won two of the next three, only to close the season with a maddening six-game losing streak. Ditka's Bears had gone an unbelievable 6–10.

The collapse was largely a defensive one, as the team slipped from No. two in '88 to No. 24 in total defense, and from No. one to No. 20 in points permitted. Moreover, the losing campaign—Ditka's first since 1982—

Dan Hampton, here sacking Dolphins quarterback Dan Marino, anchored the Bears defensive line throughout its 1980s dominance.

ended a five-year run of NFC Central championships. Despite the sorry end to the decade, it had been a strong 1980s for Chicago, with five winning seasons, five divisional crowns, and one Super Bowl. The 10-year record was a solid 92–60.

Expectations were lower among Bears fans in 1990 as Jim Harbaugh supplanted Tomczak at quarterback. The situation was made worse by a holdout by running back Neal Anderson, who had run for 1,275 yards in 1989. Anderson was retained, however, and the Bears did their usual, winning their first three games before falling to the Raiders in Los Angeles by a 24–10 count.

Now what? Bears fans wondered. Would it be another '89 brownout? It wouldn't, as Chicago's record was 9–1 before another loss occurred. The team finished 11–5, losing four of its last six and Harbaugh to a separated shoulder in a Game 14 loss at Detroit. Nonetheless, the team had taken another division title and would play the upstart New Orleans Saints in Chicago in the postseason lid-lifter.

The Bears won 16–6 and headed to New York as huge underdogs versus the Giants of Bill Parcells. The resourceful Ditka was unfazed, challenging the mighty New York defense early on a fourth-and-one for a TD. It didn't work, and neither did much else, as the Giants ended Chicago's season with a 31–3 blowout. It had been a banner season, nevertheless, with the team's defense rebounding to a sixth-ranked slot in overall defense and a No. nine rating in points allowed. Moreover, the Anderson-Harbaugh-driven offense had placed well in the upper half of the league as well—ninth in scoring and 12th overall.

Bad omens hung over the team as it opened the 1991 campaign. All-Pro tackle Jimbo Covert had back problems, while safety Shaun Gayle, another All-Pro, along with Anderson and fullback Brad Muster had leg woes. Meanwhile The Fridge had an extra compartment. He now weighed 370 pounds, negatively affecting his mobility.

And with that, the Bears won their first four games. But they did so by a combined margin of 14 points. Each game was a thriller. Steve McMichael caused a Wade Wilson interception in the opening 10–6 win over the Vikings; the team then won a 21–20 squeaker

TRIVIA

What is the critical 1992 Harbaugh interception at Minnesota often called?

Answers to the trivia questions are on pages 182–183.

1980s Bears Greats

RB Walter Payton—Sweetness always comes in first.

LB Mike Singletary—Samurai was the brains of the Bears defense and the conscience of the team. Ditka had enormous respect for the scholarly yet incredibly aggressive linebacker, often taking Christian counsel from the acknowledged team leader.

DE Richard Dent—Dent turned in a Hall of Fame level career, playing 11 years in Chicago, making four Pro Bowl squads, and being named the Super Bowl XX MVP. The eighth-round pick from Tennessee State was a pass rusher extraordinaire, credited with 124.5 sacks while with the Bears.

DL Dan Hampton—The handsome defensive lineman out of Arkansas was a six-time All-Pro who stood out at tackle and end. Called Danimal for his ferocious performances, Hampton was incredibly durable, playing through 10 knee surgeries. Danimal played in three different decades and entered the Hall of Fame in 2002.

OT Jim Covert—Payton called the Pittsburgh All-American the "best offensive tackle in the NFL." A consensus All-Rookie pick in '83, he was the Offensive Lineman of the Year in 1986. Covert was arguably the best of a tremendous cadre of offensive interior linemen during the glory years of the 1980s.

at Tampa Bay and followed that by prevailing 20–17 over the Super Bowl champion Giants in 90-degree heat when William Perry stuffed a certain field goal with seconds left. Game 4 was an overtime win at home versus the Jets, after the visitors missed an easy field goal at the end of regulation. But the team hung on. A pair of decisive losses was followed by five more wins, and the Bears were 9–2. Going into the final game at San Francisco, the Bears' record stood at 11–4. A win would give them the Central Division crown because they held the tiebreaker versus Detroit. A loss would send them into the playoffs as a wild-card. It was no contest. The 9–6 Niners blew them out 52–14.

A playoff loss to a young Cowboys team, 17–13, ended the season for Chicago. The offense penetrated the Dallas 10 on four occasions and scored a touchdown only once. It had been another 11–5 season, but Bears fans were concerned. The team was getting old and was no longer dominant, and Ditka seemed unhappy.

"I feel better about going into this season than I did in 1985," said the coach, distracting attention away from a patched-up offensive line, an aging defense (with Singletary in his final season), and no real deep threat on offense. An opening win over Detroit also had Bears fans feeling good. Three losses in the next four games soured their moods, however. The situation was made worse by an incredible event in Minnesota in Game 5. With the team up 20–0 and Ditka wanting to grind down the clock to give his charges a much-needed win in this difficult venue, Harbaugh called an audible. A pass intended for Anderson was picked off and run back for a score, and Ditka went berserk on the sideline. With the team in shock at Ditka's rage, Minnesota came back to win, 21–20.

TRIVIA

What did the Bears' media guide call the 14–13 loss at Green Bay in Game 9 of the 1989 season?

Answers to the trivia questions are on pages 182–183.

With that, Ditka faced the task of regathering his team. He did, as the Bears won the next two, setting up a Central Division showdown with the 5–2 Vikings on the lakefront.

Minnesota simply demolished the Bears, 38–10. The die was cast, and Chicago went on to drop five more in a row, leaving them at a sorry 4–9. Only a 30–6 Game 14 win over a strong Pittsburgh team in Singletary's last home game interrupted the carnage, and the Bears then lost their last two to finish 5–11.

The ice was getting thinner under Ditka, as his curious comedown continued. He complained publicly about his lack of control in personnel matters. He claimed his 1991 team was one of "overachievers," further alienating his players and members of the Bears brass, including McCaskey's personnel man, Bill Tobin. The button-down McCaskey, who never appreciated Ditka's often crude style, let the coach twist in the January wind while he went on a skiing vacation. Upon his return on January 5, he fired the coach, and the Ditka era was over.

Iron Mike

With the possible exception of George Halas, no figure in Bears lore towers over Chicago's gridiron landscape like that of Michael Keller Ditka. He is bellicose, blunt, and bigger than life. He is candid, colorful, and crass. He is kind, crude, and controversial. He is reverent, raunchy, and Runyonesque. He is witty, winning, and war-like. He is loving, lively, and lacking self-control. There is simply no one like him.

It would be easy to look at Ditka by chronicling his years at the Bears' helm—his wins, losses, and outbursts. But he invites a closer look.

What has endeared Ditka to so many Bears fans is his unabashed love for the team, his willingness to identify with the common person, and his public honesty and vulnerability. Over and over, when confronted with one of his misconducts Ditka never denied or rationalized. "I'm not proud of that," was a more common response. His only alibi was his self-acknowledged fallen nature.

Born outside of Pittsburgh on October 18, 1939, Ditka's character was burnished in coal mining country. After a brilliant, All-American, tough-guy career at Pitt, Ditka starred for the Bears before moving to the Eagles and later the Cowboys. The incisive and often inscrutable Tom Landry saw coaching potential in Ditka and kept him on his staff for nine years. It was Landry's character and football acumen that shaped the often salty-speaking Ditka's strong Christian faith and football thinking.

He came to the Bears underestimated by the football public. Viewed as a meathead who knew no strategy, people thought his fate would be indistinguishable from that of Abe Gibron. George Halas, who also had much to do with teaching the game to Iron Mike, thought differently. He saw the rough-hewn Ditka as a passionate student of the game and one

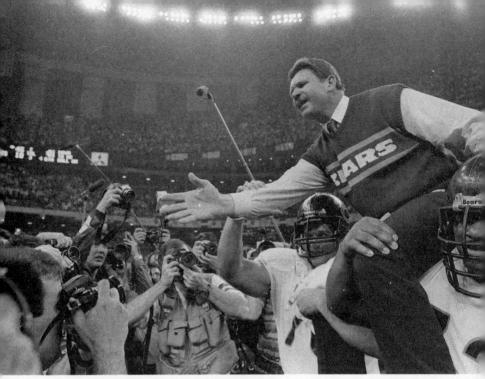

Bears players carry Mike Ditka off the field after he led them to the franchise's only Super Bowl victory, in 1986.

who understood that winning was paramount. Years later Ditka remembered his meeting with Halas when they discussed the Bears job.

> We sat down and talked. It was very informal, at the kitchen table. At the time all the fair-haired guys were coming in, the new geniuses of football. I think Mr. Halas was trying to check me out to see if I was one of them, and so he asked me what my philosophy of football was. I kind of laughed, and I said, "You know I don't think that's important. First of all, my philosophy is the same as yours. And that's strictly to win. How we do it—we have our methods and we have our ideas, but if you're asking me am I going to go out and throw the ball all over the park like it's a wounded duck, no, I'm going to play football and teach good, basic fundamentals."

And Ditka won quickly. His undoing, however, was his own monstrous ego. He was simply unable to handle his own celebrity. The world is filled with such wreckage, and Mike Ditka is just such wreckage. Once

Quotable

From the Mouth of Mike Ditka

"If you're not in the parade, you watch the parade. That's life."

"You're never a loser until you stop trying."

"Success isn't measured by money or power or social rank. Success is measured by your discipline and inner peace."

his celebrity was launched into orbit, the coach began hawking virtually every item one could peddle in a retail establishment. He opened a restaurant, appeared on television, had his own radio show, and became a street philosopher.

He soon became what is called a caricature of his own self, promoting the Iron Mike persona in interviews, commercials, and other public forums. He would make provocative statements because they drew attention and magnified his presence.

And many of his players did not like it. They saw him as trying to become larger than the players who had contributed to his success. They disliked the autocratic air in which he gloried and his promanagement stance in labor disputes. He was blessed to have humble yet incredible professionals like Walter Payton and Mike Singletary on his teams, players that could look beyond the coach's foibles. Lesser performers like Jim McMahon, who had issues of his own, could not abide Ditka and regularly feuded with him.

Nonetheless, he is a very bright man. He put together a sound offensive system, reinforced the import of a vicious defense, eliminated mistakes, and most important of all, focused his team on winning. He dominated his division and the early months of the season, leaving his opponents in pursuit before the leaves turned brown. He raised the bar of effort, demanding total and all-out passion in each player's play.

TRIVIA

In 1961 and 1962 the Bears had back-to-back Rookies of the Year. Who were they?

Answers to the trivia questions are on pages 182–183.

Furthermore, he was Lombardi-like, starting tiffs with players, making upsetting remarks about targeted players to keep his team on the edge and away from boredom. He would goad a player with a cutting comment as quickly as a pep talk, all the while knowing what he was trying to accomplish. And he accomplished much. His overabundance of ego and undersupply of self-control curtailed his effectiveness.

The Bears brass, tired of his antics, pushed Ditka out in stages. First they pulled his friend and GM, Jerry Vainisi after the '86 season, leaving no powerful figure inside the system to be his advocate. Then, rather than giving Ditka greater control of the personnel decisions, they turned to Bill Tobin. And finally, McCaskey and the other insiders waited until Ditka's star was in descent before firing him.

Mike Ditka never recovered from being fired by the Bears. After five years in broadcasting he spent an unhappy three years coaching the New Orleans Saints from 1997 to 1999 before being fired after compiling a 15–33 record. He then returned to broadcasting.

One more Super Bowl, some success in New Orleans, or a longer tenure in Chicago might have put Iron Mike in the Hall of Fame as a coach as well as a player. It didn't happen, but there is likely no coach outside the Hall better known than Iron Mike Ditka.

The Wannstedt Years

It didn't take McCaskey long to name his new coach. It was Dave Wannstedt, defensive coordinator of the Super Bowl champion Dallas Cowboys. And to sweeten the pot for the much-pursued Wannstedt, McCaskey granted the new coach control over personnel, the very issue over which Ditka had chafed ever since losing Vainisi.

With an emphasis on speed, Wannstedt reshaped the roster and readied for his opener with the Giants. A late-game 26–20 loss to the New Yorkers was followed by an inept offensive effort in a 10–7 loss at Minnesota, and Bears fans were grumbling. A blowout of Tampa Bay 47–17 backed by two more wins gave the squad a 3–2 mark. The high of the streak was followed by a three-game low, and Chicago was 3–5 at the halfway point. Just as the sky looked dark, the Bears won three straight road games and were 6–5 after 11 games. A 30–17 drubbing of the Pack made them 7–5. This up was followed by another down, however, as Chicago lost its remaining quartet of games and finished 7–9.

All in all, the early reviews of Wannstedt were positive, on the heels of the Ditka fatigue—particularly in view of the defense ranking seventh overall and third in points allowed. Work was needed on offense, however, as the Bears had no bite, ranking last overall and 24th in points scored. Wannstedt decided to turn to former Lion Erik Kramer as his quarterback, signing him as a free agent in 1994. In addition, speedster Curtis Conway was matched with Jeff Graham at the wideouts.

After a Game 3 loss to the Vikings, the team was 1–2 and without Kramer due to a shoulder injury. Backup Steve Walsh stepped in, and the team won three straight. When Kramer returned but was ineffective, Wannstedt turned again to Walsh, who had formed an effective tandem with Graham. A 4–4 team at the halfway point, the Walsh-led Bears reeled off four straight wins and the team was in the playoff hunt once more. Although losing three of their final four, the team snared the last NFC wild-card spot and headed for Minnesota to open the postseason in the Metrodome.

The Bears were the toast of the Windy City when they emerged with a lopsided 35–18 triumph. The season ended the following week with a

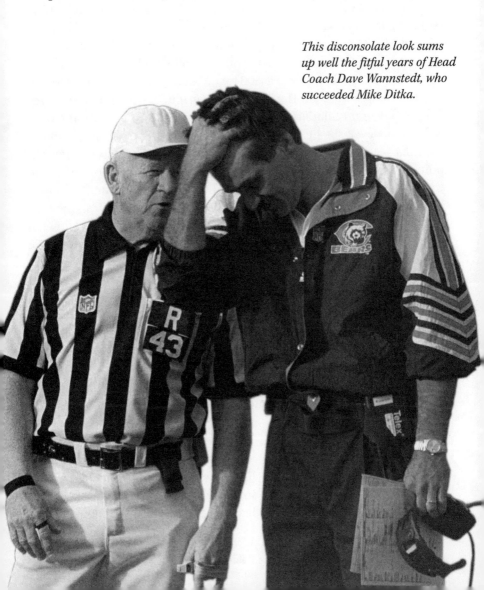

This disconsolate look sums up well the fitful years of Head Coach Dave Wannstedt, who succeeded Mike Ditka.

44–15 drubbing at the hands of the eventual Super Bowl–champion 49ers, but with Wannstedt NFC Coach of the Year, things were looking up in Chicago.

Caution should have been the watchword, however, as the 9–7 team had been outscored by 36 points in '94 and yielded 366 more yards than they had gained.

Kramer reclaimed his lost QB spot to open '95, and the team rolled to a 6–2 record at the halfway point, with Kramer having fired 18 TD strikes. The defense, however, had yielded 173 points. Three losses in which Chicago permitted 96 points followed, and playoff hopes were in jeopardy. A 27–24 win over the Giants was followed by two more losses, and suddenly the Bears were a .500 team—seven up and seven down.

The team had to get the last two. They did, 31–10 and 20–14, over Tampa Bay and Philadelphia, respectively. When Atlanta stunned the Niners, however, the Bears' playoff dream evaporated despite their 9–7 winning season. Wannstedt had fixed the offense. The team tallied 392 points, Kramer threw for more than 3,800 yards and 29 TDs, while Conway and Graham each more than 1,000 yards receiving. Moreover, despite spotty play, rookie running back Rashaan Salaam ran for over 1,000 yards. The defense, however, needed remedial work, allowing 360 points and ranking a weak 20th overall among the then 30 NFL franchises.

Money is always an issue, and it was dollars that kept Chicago from re-signing Jeff Graham in '96. They did, however, ink linebacker Brian Cox to bolster the defense. The Bears opened the season by cuffing the Super Bowl–champion Dallas Cowboys around to the tune of 22–6. Three quick losses followed, and Kramer was lost for the season with a neck injury in a 35–16 loss at Detroit. Dave Krieg, a 38-year-old veteran formerly with Seattle, took over as the injuries accumulated. The squad stumbled to a 3–5 mark at midseason and then split its last eight to finish a lackluster 7–9. The team fell 109 points in scoring offense, ranking 22nd in the league of 30. The defense improved—

TRIVIA

What comment did Wannstedt make prior to the 1996 opener with Dallas that would haunt him throughout the season?

Answers to the trivia questions are on pages 182–183.

That Mark Hatley went to the Green Bay Packers in 2001 and became vice president of football operations for the Pack after leaving the Bears? The highly regarded and much-liked Hatley died in 2004, at 54 years of age.

12th in points permitted and 11th overall. The future, particularly with Kramer's neck injury, looked uncertain.

Wannstedt made a bold move in '97, trading for struggling Rick Mirer from Seattle. Kramer was cleared by physicians to play and figured to be the starter until the former Notre Dame great was ready. Seven games into the '97 campaign, neither Mirer nor Kramer nor the Bears looked great. The team was 0–7. They lost the opener at Green Bay 38–24, amid a meltdown by Brian Cox, who was ejected after thrusting his middle finger skyward at the Green Bay crowd. A low point was experienced when the Bears lost Game 6 to the New Orleans Saints, then coached by one Mike Ditka. A come-from-behind win in Game 8 preceded losses in five of the team's final eight games to give Chicago a 4–12 record. It was a forgettable year. The team was 28th in points scored and 29th in points allowed among the 30 teams.

Wannstedt was in trouble with the fans but not with McCaskey, who stood solidly behind his coach going into '98. Personnel man Mark Hatley helped Wannstedt shuffle the deck. Gone were Mirer and Cox, and in came kick returner Glyn Milburn and Penn State rookie running back Curtis Enis.

Enis proved difficult to sign and difficult to coach and was injured in midseason. Erik Kramer was felled early and lost for the season, and the Bears once again opened dismally, losing their first four. They then won three of four, but now weak on both sides of the ball, the Bears went 1–7 in the second half, and it was 4–12 once again.

McCaskey was now waffling on Wannstedt, saying near season's end, "Every member of this organization will be held to a high standard and will be reviewed at the end of the year."

McCaskey, oldest son of Halas's daughter, Virginia, had problems of his own. He actually had little chance to succeed as the man in charge of the Bears. He was immensely unpopular in many quarters for firing the beloved Ditka, and the dislike was compounded by his support of the beleaguered Dave Wannstedt.

More important, perhaps, was the politics of style. Holder of a doctorate in business from Case Western Reserve University and having taught at Harvard's Business School, McCaskey had an aristocratic mien, one that grated on the cultural nerves of the Bears faithful, a mass that celebrated blue-collar values, football, and style.

Although many felt McCaskey would spare Wannstedt and shake up his staff, instead on January 28 the 47-year-old coach was dismissed. Despite a solid start, Wannstedt finished with a 41–57 record, falling far short of icon Ditka's 112–68 mark.

A Quiet, Polite, and Gracious Man

The search for a new coach began with a comedy of errors. The job was offered to Dave McGinniss, a popular candidate. Given that this was McGinniss's dream job, having coached under Ditka and Wannstedt, the Bears were confident that he would accept, although McGinniss told McCaskey he had to think about it. The Bears set up a 1:00 press conference the following day to announce McGinniss as the new coach. The would-be coach was offended by the presumptuous actions of the Bears and backed out, leaving the organization without a new coach and much egg on its face.

McCaskey hastened through the short list Hatley had tendered him and quickly offered the position to 49-year-old Dick Jauron. Unlike Wannstedt, Jauron had played the game. He had been a defensive back for eight years in the NFL and made one Pro Bowl squad. A quiet, polite, and gracious man, Jauron was unafraid to make bold moves. He began by installing Gary Crowton of Louisiana Tech as his offensive coordinator. The move was questioned by some because Crowton was known for a wide-open offense, typical of the college game he coached.

Hatley got the quarterback he wanted out of the draft, Cade McNown of UCLA. When the Bears released Kramer, however, it left only Shane Matthews and the untested and unsigned McNown to play the position. Matthews, as well as running back Enis, proved effective, although the team managed only an opening day win among its first three games. The team then won a pair, including a comeback triumph over the New Orleans Saints on the strength of two Matthews-to-Conway TD strikes and a win at Minnesota. The win in the Metrodome was costly, however, as Matthews was left limping due to a bad hamstring pull. An unprepared McNown quarterbacked losses in the next two games, and when Matthews was still gimpy in the Washington game, the rookie returned for another humiliation. The Bears were 3–5 at the halfway point.

Out of nowhere came Jim Miller late in the season, passing for more than 400 yards twice and more than 300 once. Miller, however, was banished after Game 12 for taking a generic supplement that was on the NFL outlaw list, and the team dropped three of its final four to finish at 6–10.

The 1990s were nothing like the '80s. It looked like a return to the 1970s as the team won just 73 games and lost 87, with only four winning seasons, but none after 1995. There was guarded enthusiasm as the new millennium approached.

Hatley was hard at work improving team speed in the off-season, and as 2000 approached, Bears fans were enthusiastic.

Anthony Thomas, here running through the arms of Raiders lineman Dana Stubblefield, showed signs early in his career of becoming the next great Bears running back.

It didn't last long. Cade McNown, tabbed as the No. one quarterback by Jauron, was a bust. The team won only one of its first eight games, and the fans were howling for Miller to take over under center. He finally got his

TRIVIA

For which two teams did Jauron play?

Answers to the trivia questions are on pages 182–183.

chance when McNown was banged up in Game 8, a 13–9 loss to the Eagles. His chance did not last long. After leading the team to a big win over the powerful Colts, 27–24, Miller tore his achilles the next week in a 20–3 loss at Buffalo. The forgotten Shane Matthews was the main man the rest of the way, as the Bears split their final six games for a sorry 5–11 finish. The team ranked 24th on overall offense, 28th in points scored among the 31 NFL teams.

With new president Phillips staunchly supporting Jauron, 2001 dawned with bridled enthusiasm. In the spring, however, Mark Hatley left upon completing the draft, and the Bears searched for his replacement. The job went to Jerry Angelo, who was named GM. Despite his late start, Angelo did his share of dealing, mainly cutting salaries off the payroll, although many felt he was all but dooming Jauron with a poor team. In fact, Jauron's days did figure to be numbered, as he was not the new GM's choice.

A grinding 17–6 loss at Baltimore to the Super Bowl–champion Ravens opened the season. Despite losing Shane Matthews in their second game, the team roared back after trailing 10–0 at the half to win 17–10. With that the team really pulled together, streaking to five straight wins. Despite a 20–12 loss to the Packers at home, the team closed the first half with a 6–2 mark.

The first half had been sweet. After Jim Miller was hurt against San Francisco, Matthews rallied the squad from a 28–9 third-quarter deficit to push the game into overtime. When Mike Brown picked off an errant 49ers pass and returned it for six, the Chicago fans exploded. One week later, the Bears scored twice against Cleveland with under a minute left, to go into overtime again, tied at 21. Believe it or not, Mike Brown intercepted a pass again and took it home for the win.

Though only slightly less dramatic, the second half of the campaign was even more successful, as the team won seven of eight to hang a 13–3 record, the best Bears season in 15 years. Although the team ranked 27th in

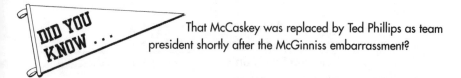

overall offense, they were 11th in scoring (338 points). The defense allowed the fewest points of any team (203), although standing 12th overall.

Anthony "A-Train" Thomas had a banner rookie season, piling up 1,183 yards and seven TDs on the ground.

Andy Reid's 11–5 Eagles visited Soldier Field as substantial underdogs to the Bears in the playoff opener. They didn't play like it, though. Hugh Douglas knocked Jim Miller out of the game on a questionable hit and the Eagles never looked back, winning 33–19.

It didn't matter. The Bears were back under Coach of the Year Dick Jauron.

With Soldier Field being renovated in 2002, the team moved its home games south to the University of Illinois, in Champaign-Urbana. If enthusiasm was rampant in the preseason, it hit its peak after the Bears copped wins in each of their first two games.

The Bears then blew a 20–0 lead against New Orleans en route to a horrendous eight-game losing streak. Six of the eight defeats were by six points or less. It made no difference. The season was pretty much over with six games still remaining. The team never turned it around, winning only two of the games (one in overtime versus the Lions) to finish 4–12.

In 2003 Angelo turned up the heat on his coach, stating that he expected to have the Bears in the playoffs at season's end. In search of a quarterback, Angelo courted Jake Plummer of the Arizona Cardinals, but after being rebuffed had to settle for the mercurial Kordell Stewart, from the Pittsburgh Steelers. Stewart was a gifted runner with a howitzer arm but who lacked the finesse to run an offense effectively. Hence he had been released by Pittsburgh. The Bears let Miller go, not surprising due to his injury-plagued tenure in Chicago.

The season's inaugural game was played in San Francisco, where a depleted offensive line and an inept defense contributed to a 49–7 shellacking. Two more losses followed until the team registered a victory over the struggling Oakland Raiders on a last-second field goal, 24–21. Two tight defeats followed, and Jauron inserted veteran Chris Chandler in relief of Stewart. The club moved its record up to 3–5 on the strength of a pair of wins. A pair of agonizing two-point losses drove the team's record down to 3–7—all but out of it for Angelo-expected playoffs.

Two impressive victories were next, and with only four games left, Jauron's future was a matter of public debate. He didn't exactly have the horses, but then again, four losing seasons in five attempts do not a successful NFL coach make. Two more wins and two more losses closed the books on another unsatisfying 7–9 season.

A day after the season ended Angelo announced that Jauron was being let go because "expectations were not met." Fans were not in total accord on the firing. Jauron had been a stand-up guy for whom the players played hard. He had tried to swim in a shallow pool of talent. And perhaps most of all, he may have finished last, but he was indeed a nice guy.

A Love Feast

The 2004 season brought the Bears their 13th coach and first African American mentor, Lovie Smith, formerly the defensive coordinator of the St. Louis Rams. Lovie's tenure started with a whimper rather than a bang, coaching a team with many new faces. An exciting 21–10 victory in Green Bay in the season's second game, one in which Lovie made immediate good on his No. one stated goal upon being hired—to beat Green Bay—was followed by four straight losses. A 19–17 win at Tennessee in Game 9 pushed the team to a 4–5 mark, and playoff chatter could be heard throughout Chicago. It was short-lived, as the team skidded to a 1–6 finish, two games behind the deposed Jauron's 2003 contingent that went 7–9.

The team mounted no offense, ranking dead last (32nd) in points scored and total offense. The Bears scored just 10 touchdowns on the ground and nine in the air. GM Jerry Angelo peddled top receiver Marty Booker in the off-season, and Rex Grossman, anointed as the team's No. one quarterback, was gone for the season by the third game, owing to a knee injury on the Minnesota turf. None of the three successors to Grossman—Jonathan Quinn, Craig Krenzel, or Chad Hutchinson— played well enough to make the roster even a year later. Amazingly, it was an offensive performer, center Olin Kreutz, who was the team's lone Pro Bowl selection.

The defense was hampered in particular by two injuries. Ace safety Mike Brown tore an Achilles tendon in the win against the Packers and Brian Urlacher was dogged throughout the season with a bad hamstring. Fortunately for Smith it was only his first year at the Bears throttle and the even-tempered mentor benefited from the traditional honeymoon period accorded new coaches.

The 2005 season carried with it some demands. Fans were becoming restless after three straight losing seasons, eight in the last nine, and the public heat began to be turned up on GM Angelo and his still unproven new coach. That Smith had no previous head coaching experience, as was the case with every one of his post-Halas predecessors, offered him little in the way of political traction among disgruntled fans and an ever more cynical media, and Angelo faced constant criticism on the personnel front.

Opening the season with a dull 9–7 loss at Washington did nothing to quiet the critics. Much of the furor began in the preseason when the yet unproven No. one quarterback Grossman was lost for the bulk of the season with a leg injury and Angelo was caught devoid of a solid veteran backup to salvage the season. As it turned out, fourth-round draft choice Kyle Orton was handed the reins over journeyman and recent pickup Jeff Blake. In any case, a loss in which the Bears managed only seven points looked like more of the 2004 same to unhappy Chicago fans.

A surprising 38–6 Soldier Field rout of the Detroit Lions followed, but few Bears followers took much comfort in a win over the doormat Detroiters. When a 20–10 road loss to lowly Cleveland followed a 24–7 home defeat at the hands of the up-and-coming Cincinnati Bengals, the Bears were 1–3, with many observers marking time on Lovie Smith. The mere 24 points in three losses had many believing Smith had no offensive answer in the face of sophisticated NFL defenses, and hence the Bears and Lovie were doomed.

A 28–3 pummeling of the troubled Vikings in Soldier Field was a feel-good experience for Bears fans, but nothing over which to become excited. When the defense yielded just six points to the visiting Ravens in a 10–6 triumph, the Bears pulled to the .500 line and the team's scintillating defense began getting more positive coverage than the offense did negative attention. A date in Detroit followed, and the Lions, tougher this time, did not have enough to stop the Chicagoans from posting a 19–13 win.

Two more victories followed, but against the NFL underclass, New Orleans and San Francisco. The 6–3 Bears, with Orton at least not losing games under center, were due to play host to the Carolina Panthers, a winning team that would provide a yardstick by which Bears fans could measure their team's true quality. When the Bears emerged with a 13–3

TRIVIA

**Who was the Bears'
No. one draft
choice in 2005?**

Answers to the trivia questions are on pages 182–183.

victory, optimism abounded. The team
was 7–3, three—perhaps two—games
from being playoff timber. Better yet,
their division, the NFL North, was weak.
Green Bay was injured and inept, the
Vikings self-destructive and losing, and
the hapless Lions were soon to fire Steve
Mariucci in favor of ex-Bears mentor Dick Jauron.

Doubts really began to vanish when the Bears returned from Tampa
Bay 13–10 winners over the playoff-bound Buccaneers. The defense was
all the rage, having allowed just 120 points in 11 games. Comparisons
with the '85 juggernaut, one that permitted just 198 points for the
season, were now commonplace on talk radio and in the papers. A 19–7
conquest of the hated Packers only turned up the volume on praise for
the Chicago defense. Meanwhile Orton, while certainly not "making
plays" at quarterback, was quietly showing he could manage the
offense—one among the elite in rushing—well enough to win consistently while Grossman was on the verge of being pronounced fit to play
again.

A 21–9 pounding in Pittsburgh, however, raised questions. Was the
Bears bubble about to burst? With the Vikings coming on, might a losing
streak now be setting in, robbing the team of a divisional title? Was
Orton's good fortune about to end in the ashes of a stuffed ground game?

The Bears rallied with a 16–3 win over Michael Vick and the Atlanta
Falcons. Smith risked creating a quarterback controversy by starting
Grossman in the second half over a struggling Orton. Grossman threw
with authority, and the offense perked up while the defense dominated
the men from the South. Smith wasted no time resolving any QB controversy by naming Grossman the main man for the remainder of the
season. He and his mates responded with a 24–17 verdict in Green Bay,
giving the Bears a season sweep and Smith a 3–1 record against the Pack.

All was well. The Bears were 11–4, champions of the North, and mer-
iting a bye in the first round of the playoffs. In a somewhat bizarre move,
however, Smith decided to sit Grossman out in the finale in Minneapolis,
and the Bears closed the season on the short end of a 34–10 count. Fans
were divided on that quarterback call. Many felt strongly that the still-
rusty Grossman needed to take as many game snaps as possible,

A LOVE FEAST

Lovie Smith, here in 2006, restored the bite in the Bears by leading them to the division title in 2005.

All-Time Bears

Linebackers (listed alphabetically)

Doug Buffone—Played 14 solid seasons (1966–1979) for the Bears, much in the shadow of Butkus, captaining the defense for eight of them.

Dick Butkus—Bigger-than-life gridiron figure, Hall of Fame Butkus played on eight Pro Bowl teams in his nine-year career.

George Connor—Legendary Notre Dame star was as famous as a linebacker as he was in the offensive line.

Joe Fortunato—Great outside linebacker during the defense-dominated 1950s and '60s, was on five Pro Bowl teams.

Bill George—Underrated Hall of Fame middle linebacker for some of the greatest Bears defenses of all time; eight times in the Pro Bowl, beginning in his third season (1954).

Bronko Nagurski—Absolutely legendary figure of Bears lore. Despite his greatness at fullback, was a virtual snowplow at offensive tackle and a truly bone-crushing linebacker during his nine-year, five-time All-Pro career.

Mike Singletary—"Samurai" was the soul of the Bears' defense in the Ditka era; Hall of Fame and nine times All-NFC, he was twice Defensive Player of the Year.

Bulldog Turner—Linebacker extraordinaire as well as offensive center, led league in interceptions in 1942 and played on four NFL champions in a Hall of Fame career.

Brian Urlacher—Defensive Player of the Year in 2005, Urlacher was named to the Pro Bowl squad in five of his first six seasons.

Otis Wilson—Bear from 1980 to 1987 and part of the great Ryan defense at outside linebacker, was Pro Bowl pick in the championship 1985 season.

particularly with a week off prior to the playoffs. Others recounted his injury on the Minnesota turf in 2004, and so agreed with Lovie's strategy to keep him safe.

The 34-point barrage left the Bears four points behind the 1985 points-allowed standard of 198. Overall, the defense ranked No. two in the NFL, while the offense came in second to last. Despite winning 11 games, the Bears scored only 58 more points than their opponents. No matter, the fans were delirious, and the Super Bowl was on their lips as the playoffs began. The Carolina Panthers, 23–0 winners over the Giants in the wild-card opening round, would be the Bears' first postseason opponents.

Soldier Field was electric with excitement. The Bears were only two wins from going back to the Super Bowl in this, the 20th anniversary of the 1985 championship. What figured to be a defensive battle turned out to be a 50-point affair. The bad news for the Bears was that Carolina scored 29 of those 50.

The sadness was temporary. Lovie had created a love feast for Bears fans, who savored the surprisingly successful season, as well as high hopes for the future. The dominating defense, led by Defensive Player of the Year Brian Urlacher, promised to remain strong for years to come, while the offense—with Thomas Jones racking up 1,335 yards on the ground and Grossman showing flashes of brilliance—figured to improve.

Another exciting Bears era was underway.

ANSWERS TO
TRIVIA QUESTIONS

Page 2: George Halas played defensive end.

Page 4: They are the colors of George Halas's alma mater, the University of Illinois.

Page 9: The Hall of Fame is located on George Halas Drive.

Page 19: Cardinals star Paddy Driscoll later coached the Chicago Bears.

Page 27: The title of the movie serial Red Grange made in the 1920s was *The Galloping Ghost.*

Page 34: The Bears selected University of Chicago Heisman Trophy winner Jay Berwanger, but he never played for Chicago.

Page 37: Bears fans called Bill Hewitt the Off-Side Kid and his teammates nicknamed him Stinky.

Page 40: Sid Luckman played halfback, because he had difficulty with the quickness and complexity of the T formation offense.

Page 47: The Packers had a five-pound sack of horse manure delivered to the Bears' locker room before a 1984 game.

Page 52: Bernie Masterson was the Bears' regular quarterback before Sid Luckman took over.

Page 53: The Japanese bombed Pearl Harbor.

Page 74: The NFL owners were very happy when the league set an attendance record, drawing 1,732,135 fans, for a very healthy 31,494-per-game average.

Page 81: Numbers were retired for the following Bears greats: Nagurski—3, Turner—66, McAfee—5, and Luckman—42.

Page 88: Curly Lambeau was the Cardinals coach in 1950 and 1951.

Page 95: Driscoll was 60 when he took over for Halas as Bears coach.

Page 98: After constant wranglings with Halas, Doug Atkins was sent to the New Orleans Saints, where he was a standout for three years. He was 39 when he retired.

Page 101: George Allen was the Bears assistant who put together the successful zone defense in 1963.

Page 102: Ronnie Bull of Baylor was the Bears 1962 Rookie of the Year.

Page 107: Virgil Carter led the Bears to four straight wins in 1968, before breaking his leg.

Page 109: Quarterback Jack Concannon came to the Bears in 1967 in exchange for Mike Ditka.

Page 111: Jeannie Morris, then wife of Bears receiver Johnny Morris, wrote the popular book titled *Brian Piccolo: A Short Season.*

Page 113: Brian Piccolo attended Wake Forest University.

Page 121: Rookie Cecil Turner, from Cal Poly-San Luis Obispo, returned four kickoffs for touchdowns, tying an NFL record and making the NFC Pro Bowl team in the process.

Page 122: Bobby Douglass and Gale Sayers both went to the University of Kansas.

Page 127: The Bears acquired former Viking Alan Page in October 1978.

Page 128: Dick Vermeil was the coach of the Eagles in the 1979 playoff game.

Page 131: Jim Brown ran for 12,312 yards to hold the career rushing record before Walter Payton.

Page 140: The day after the loss to the Dolphins a number of players recorded "The Super Bowl Shuffle."

Page 145: Al Harris and Todd Bell sat out all of 1985 and thus missed a Super Bowl season.

Page 149: Buddy Ryan's real first name is James.

Page 150: In Game 12 of 1986, the Packers' Charles Martin slammed McMahon to the turf in an obvious cheap shot, ending the quarterback's season.

Page 155: Against Minnesota in 1977 Walter Payton gained 275 rushing yards.

Page 159: The critical 1992 Harbaugh interception at Minnesota is often called "The Play."

Page 161: The Bears' media guide called the Game 9 loss at Green Bay in 1989 the Instant Replay Game, because a later penalty against Packers QB Don Majkowski for throwing beyond the line of scrimmage was reversed by replay and a TD awarded.

Page 164: Mike Ditka and Ronnie Bull were Bears back-to-back Rookie of the Year winners in 1961 and 1962.

Page 169: Dave Wannstedt said, "All the pieces are in place to make a deep run into the playoffs," a comment that would haunt him throughout the season.

Page 173: Dick Jauron played for the Detroit Lions and Cincinnati Bengals.

Page 178: Cedric Benson was the Bears' No. one draft choice in 2005.

Chicago Bears
All-Time Roster
(through 2005)

Roster includes players who have appeared in at least one game with the Chicago Bears.

A

Abbey, Joe (North Texas State) E	1948–49
Abdullah, Rabih (Lehigh) RB	2002–03
Abraham, Clifton (Florida State) CB	1996
Adamle, Mike (Northwestern) RB	1975–76
Adams, John (Los Angeles State) B	1959–62
Adams, Scott (Georgia) T	1995
Adickes, John (Baylor) C	1987–88
Adkins, Roy (Millikin & Bethany) G	1920–21
Age, Louis (SW Louisiana) T	1992
Aguiar, Louie (Utah State) P	2000
Akin, Len (Baylor) G	1942
Albrecht, Ted (California) T	1977–81
Allen, Duane (Santa Ana) E	1966–67
Allen, Eddie (Pennsylvania) FB	1947
Allen, Egypt (TCU) DB	1987
Allen, James (Oklahoma) RB	1998–2001
Allen, Tremayne (Florida) TE	1997–98
Allman, Robert (Michigan State) E	1936
Allred, John (USC) TE	1997–2000
Althoff, Jim (Winona State) DT	1987
Amsler, Marty (Evansville) DE	1967–68
Anderson, Art (Idaho) T	1961–62
Anderson, Brad (Arizona) WR	1984–85
Anderson, Bryan (Pittsburgh) G	2004
Anderson, Ed (Notre Dame) E	1923
Anderson, Henry (Northwestern) G	1931
Anderson, Hunk (Notre Dame) G	1922–27
Anderson, Ken (Arkansas) DT	1999
Anderson, Marcus (Tulane) WR	1981
Anderson, Neal (Florida) RB	1986–93
Anderson, Ralph (Los Angeles State) E	1958
Anderson, William (Compton JC) HB	1953–54
Andrews, Tom (Louisville) C	1984–85
Antoine, Lionel (Southern Illinois) T	1972–77
Apolskis, Charles (DePaul) E	1938–39
Ardizzone, Tony (Northwestern) C	1979
Armstrong, Trace (Florida) DT	1989–94
Arnett, Jon (USC) HB	1964–66
Arp, John (Lincoln) T	1987
Artoe, Lee (California) T	1940–43
Ashburn, Clifford (Nebraska) T	1930
Asher, Bob (Vanderbilt) T	1972–75
Ashmore, M. Roger (Gonzaga) T	1927
Aspatore, Edward (Marquette) T	1934
Atkins, Doug (Tennessee) E	1955–66
Atkins, Kelvin (Illinois) LB	1983
Austin, Ray (Tennessee) S	1998–99
Austin, Reggie (Wake Forest) CB	2001–02
Autrey, Billy (SF Austin) C	1953
Autry, Darnell (Northwestern) RB	1997
Auzenne, Troy (California) T	1992–95
Avellini, Bob (Maryland) QB	1975–84
Aveni, John (Indiana) E	1959–60
Ayanbadejo, Brendon (UCLA) LB	2005
Azumah, Jerry (New Hampshire) CB	1999–2005

B

Babartsky, Al (Fordham) T	1943–45
Babinecz, John (Villanova) LB	1975
Badaczewski, J. (Western Reserve) G	1953
Bailey, Johnny (Texas A & I) WR	1990–91
Baisi, Al (West Virginia) G	1940–41, 1946
Baker, Myron (Louisiana Tech) LB	1993–95
Banks, Fred (Liberty) WR	1993
Barker, Richard (Iowa State) G	1921
Barnes, Erich (Purdue) HB	1958–60
Barnes, Gary (Clemson) E	1964
Barnes, Joe (Texas Tech) QB	1974
Barnes, Lew (Oregon) WR	1986
Barnes, Marlon (Colorado) RB	2000
Barnett, Steve (Oregon) T	1963
Barnhardt, Tom (North Carolina) P	1987
Bartholomew, Brent (Ohio State) P	2000
Barwegan, Richard (Purdue) G	1950–52
Baschnagel, Brian (Ohio State) WR	1976–84
Bass, Robert (Miami–FL) LB	1995
Bassi, Dick (Santa Clara) G	1938–39
Bates, D'Wayne (Northwestern) WR	1999–2001
Battles, Bill (Brown) E	1939
Bauman, Alf (Northwestern) T	1948–50
Bausch, Frank (Kansas) C	1937–40
Baxter, Fred (Auburn) TE	2001–02
Baynham, Craig (Georgia Tech) RB	1970
Becker, Dave (Iowa) S	1980
Becker, Doug (Notre Dame) LB	1978
Becker, Kurt (Michigan) G	1982–89
Becker, Wayland (Marquette) E	1934
Bell, Bob (Missouri) LB	1987
Bell, Kay (Washington State) T	1937
Bell, Ricky (NC State) CB	1997–98
Bell, Todd (Ohio State) S	1981–84, 1986
Belton, Thump (Syracuse) FB	2005
Benjamin, Ryan (South Florida) C	2001
Bennett, Ben (Duke) QB	1987
Bennett, Edgar (Florida State) RB	1998–99
Benson, Cedric (Texas) RB	2005
Benton, Jim (Arkansas) E	1943
Berger, Mitch (Colorado) P	1995
Bergerson, Gilbert (Oregon State) G	1932–33
Berlin, Eddie (Northern Iowa) WR	2005
Berrian, Bernard (Fresno State) WR	2004–05
Berry, Connie, M. (NC State) E	1942–46
Berry, Royce (Houston) DE	1976
Best, Art (Kent State) RB	1977–78
Bettis, Tom (Purdue) LB	1963
Bettridge, John (Ohio State) HB	1937
Bingham, Don (Sul Ross) HB	1956
Bishop, Bill (North Texas) T	1952–60
Bishop, Don (Los Angeles City) E	1959
Bivins, Charles (Morris Brown) HB	1960–66
Bjork, Del (Oregon) T	1937–38
Blackburn, J. A. (no college) T	1923
Blacklock, Hugh (Michigan State) T	1920–25
Blackman, Lennon (Tulsa) HB	1930
Blackwell, Kelly (TCU) TE	1992
Blair, Paul (Oklahoma State) T	1986–87
Blake, Jeff (East Carolina) QB	2005
Blanda, George (Kentucky) QB–K	1949–58
Blaylock, Anthony (Winston–Salem) CB	1993
Boden, Lynn (South Dakota State) G	1979
Bolan, George (Purdue) FB	1921–24
Bonderant, J. B. (DePaul) C	1922
Boniol, Chris (Louisiana Tech) K	1999
Booker, Marty (NW Louisiana) WR	1999–2003
Boone, Alfonso (Mt. San Antonio JC) DT	2001–05
Boone, J. R. (Tulsa) HB	1948–51
Bortz, Mark (Iowa) G	1983–94
Boso, Cap (Illinois) TE	1987–91
Bowers, Sam (Fordham) TE	1987
Bownes, Fabien (W. Illinois) WR	1995–98
Brackett, M. L. (Auburn) T	1956–57
Bradley, Chuck (Oregon) TE	1977
Bradley, Ed (Wake Forest) G	1950, 1952
Bradley, Mark (Oklahoma) WR	2005
Bradley, Steve (Indiana) QB	1987
Bragg, Craig (UCLA) WR	2005
Braidwood, Charles (Chattanooga) E	1932
Bramhall, Art (DePaul) HB	1931
Bratkowski, Zeke (Georgia) QB	1954, 1957–60, 1972
Bray, Ray (Western Michigan) G	1939–42, 1946–51

Brewer, Chris (Arizona) RB	1987	Butterfield, Mark (Stanford) QB	1996
Briggs, Greg (Texas Southern) LB	1996	Buzin, Rich (Penn State) T	1972
Briggs, Lance (Arizona) LB	2003–05		
Brink, Larry (Northern Illinois) E	1954	**C**	
Britton, Earl (Illinois) FB	1925	Cabral, Brian (Colorado) LB	1981–85
Brockermeyer, Blake (Texas) T	1999–2001	Cadile, James (San Jose State) G	1962–72
Brockman, Edward (Oklahoma) B	1930	Caffey, Lee Roy (Texas A&M) LB	1970
Brooks, Anthony (E. Texas State) WR	1993	Cain, Jeremy (Massachusetts) LB	2004–05
Brooks, Macey (James Madison) WR	1999–2000	Cain, Joe (Oregon Tech) LB	1993–96
Brown, Alex (Florida) DE	2002–05	Caldwell, Mike (Middle Tennessee State) LB	2002
Brown, Charlie (Syracuse) DB	1966–67	Calland, Lee (Louisville) CB	1969
Brown, Ed (San Francisco) QB	1954–61	Cameron, Jack (Winston–Salem) WR	1984
Brown, Kevin (W. Texas State) P	1987	Campana, Al (Youngstown) HB	1950–53
Brown, Mike (Nebraska) S	2000–05	Campbell, Gary (Colorado) LB	1977–83
Brown, Ruben (Pittsburgh) G	2004–05	Campbell, Leon (Arkansas) FB	1952–54
Brown, William (Illinois) FB	1961	Canady, James (Texas) HB	1948–49
Bruer, Bob (Mankato State) TE	1976	Carey, Bob (Michigan State) E	1958
Brumbaugh, Carl (Florida) QB	1930–37	Carl, Harland (Wisconsin) HB	1956
Brupbacher, Ross (Texas A&M) LB	1970–73	Carlson, Jules "Zuck" (Oregon State) G	1929–36
Bryan, Johnny (Chicago) HB	1922–25	Caroline, J. C. (Illinois) HB	1956–65
Bryant, Waymond (Tennessee State) LB	1974–77	Carrier, Mark (USC) S	1990–96
Buck, Arthur (John Carroll) HB	1941	Carter, Daryl (Wisconsin) LB	1997
Buckler, William "Bill" (Alabama) G	1926–31	Carter, Marty (Mid. Tenn. State) S	1995–98
Buffone, Doug (Louisville) LB	1966–79	Carter, Tom (Notre Dame) CB	1997–99
Buford, Maury (Texas Tech) P	1985–86, 1989–91	Carter, Tony (Minnesota) RB	1994–97
Buivid, Ray (Marquette) QB–HB	1937–38	Carter, Virgil (BYU) QB	1968–69, 1976–77
Bukich, Rudy (USC) QB	1958–59, 1962–68	Casares, Rick (Florida) FB	1955–64
Bull, Ronnie (Baylor) B	1962–70	Casey, Tim (Oregon) LB	1969
Burdick, Lloyd (Illinois) T	1931–32	Cash, Kerry (Texas) TE	1996
Burgeis, Glenn (Tulsa) T	1945	Castete, Jesse (McNeese State) HB	1956
Burger, Todd (Penn State) G	1993–97	Cerqua, Marq (Carson–Newman College) LB	2002
Burks, Randy (SE Oklahoma State) WR	1976	Chamberlin, Guy (Nebraska) E	1920–21
Burman, George (Northwestern) T	1964	Chambers, Wally (E Kentucky) DT	1973–77
Burns, Keith (Oklahoma State) LB	1999	Chancey, Robert (no college) FB	1998
Burris, Henry (Temple) QB	2002	Chandler, Chris (Washington) QB	2002–03
Burton, James (Fresno State) CB	1994–97	Chapura, Dick (Missouri) DT	1987–89
Burton, Shane (Tennessee) DT	1999	Chesley, Al (Pittsburgh) LB	1982
Buss, Arthur (Michigan State) T	1934–35	Chesney, Chester "Chet" (DePaul) C	1939–40
Bussey, Young (LSU) QB	1940–41	Childs, Clarence (Florida A&M) DB	1968
Butkus, Dick (Illinois) LB	1965–73	Christian, Bob (Northwestern) FB	1992–94
Butler, Gary (Rice) TE	1975	Cifers, Ed (Tennessee) E	1947–48
Butler, Kevin (Georgia) K	1985–95	Clark, Darryl (Texas) RB	1987

Clark, Desmond (Wake Forest) TE	2003–05
Clark, Gail (Michigan State) LB	1973
Clark, Greg (Arizona State) LB	1988
Clark, Harry (West Virginia) HB	1940–43
Clark, Herman (Oregon State) G	1952–56
Clark, Jon (Temple) T	1996–97
Clark, Phil (Northwestern) DB	1970
Clarkson, Stuart (Texas A&I) G	1942, 1946–50
Clemons, Craig (Iowa) S	1972–77
Coady, Rich (Memphis State) C/E	1970–74
Cobb, Mike (Michigan State) TE	1978–81
Cobb, Trevor (Rice) RB	1994
Cody, Ed (Purdue) FB	1949–50
Coia, Angelo (USC) HB	1960–63
Cole, Emerson (Toledo) FB	1952
Cole, Linzy (TCU) WR	1970
Coleman, Travis (Hampton) DB	2002
Coley, James (Clemson) TE	1990
Collier, Ervin (Florida A & M) DT	1995
Collins, Andre (Penn State) LB	1998
Colombo, Marc (Boston College) T	2002, 2004
Colvin, Rosevelt (Purdue) LB	1999–2002
Concannon, Jack (Boston College) QB	1967–71
Conkright, Bill (Oklahoma) C	1937–38
Connor, George (Notre Dame) T	1948–55
Conway, Curtis (USC) WR	1993–99
Conzelman, Jim (Washington) HB	1920
Cook, Marv (Iowa) TE	1994
Cooke, Ed (Maryland) E	1958
Copeland, Ron (UCLA) WR	1969
Corbett, George (Millikin) HB	1932–38
Cornish, Frank (Grambling) DT	1966–70
Corzine, Lester (Davis & Elkins) HB	1938
Cotton, Craig (Youngstown) TE	1973
Cousin, Terry (South Carolina) CB	1997–99
Covert, Jim (Pittsburgh) T	1983–90
Cowan, Les (McMurry) T	1951
Cox, Bryan (W. Illinois) LB	1996–97
Cox, Ron (Fresno State) LB	1990–95, 1997
Crawford, Fred (Duke) T	1934–35
Crawford, James "Mush" (Illinois) G	1925
Croft, Abe (SMU) E	1944–45

Croftcheck, Don (Indiana) G	1967
Cross, Bob (SF Austin State) T	1952–53
Culpepper, Brad (Florida) DT	2000
Culver, Alvin (Notre Dame) T	1932
Cunningham, Harold (Ohio State) E	1929
Curchin, Jeff (Florida State) T	1970–71
Currie, Airese (Clemson) WR	2005

D

Daffer, Ted (Tennessee) E	1954
Damore, John (Northwestern) C	1957–58
Daniell, Jim (Ohio State) T	1945
Daniels, Dick (Pacific–Oregon) S	1969–70
Daniels, Phillip (Georgia) DE	2000–03
Davis, Art (Alabama State) T	1953–54
Davis, Fred (Alabama) T	1946–51
Davis, Harper (Old Miss) HB	1950
Davis, John (Missouri) DB	1970
Davis, John (Emporia State) TE	2001–02
Davis, Rashied (San Jose State) CB	2005
Davis, Rob (Shippensburg – PA) DT–LS	1996
Davis, Roger (Syracuse) G	1960–63
Davis, Russell (North Carolina) DE	1999
Davis, Wendell (LSU) WR	1988–93
Dean, Fred (Texas Southern) G	1977
DeCorrevont, Bill (Northwestern) HB	1948–49
DeLong, Steve (Tennessee) DE	1972
Deloplaine, Jack (Salem) RB	1979
Dempsey, Frank (Florida) G	1950–53
Denney, Austin (Tennessee) E	1967–69
Denson, Autrey (Notre Dame) RB	2001
Dent, Richard (Tennessee State) DE	1983–93, 1995
Devlin, Chris (Penn State) LB	1978
Dewveall, Willard (SMU) E	1959–60
Digris, Bernie (Holy Cross) T	1943
Dimancheff, Boris "Babe" (Purdue) HB	1952
Ditka, Mike (Pittsburgh) TE	1961–66
Dodd, Al (NW Louisiana) DB	1967
Doehring, John "Bull" (no college) FB	1932–37
Doerger, Jerry (Wisconsin) T	1982
Dogins, Kevin (Texas A&M–Kingsville) C	2001–02

Donchez, Tom (Penn State) RB	1975	Enis, Curtis (Penn State) RB	1998–2000
Dooley, Jim (Miami Florida) E	1952–54, 1956–57,	Epps, Tory (Memphis State) DT	1993–94
	1959–62	Erickson, Harold (Washington & Jefferson) HB	1925
Dottley, John (Mississippi) FB	1951–53	Evans, Earl (Harvard) T	1926–29
Douglas, Merrill (Utah) FB	1958–60	Evans, Fred (Notre Dame) HB	1948
Douglass, Bobby (Kansas) QB	1969–75	Evans, Vince (USC) QB	1977–83
Douglass, Maurice (Kentucky) DB	1986–93	Evey, Dick (Tennessee) T	1964–69
Douthitt, Earl (Iowa) S	1975		
Dowden, Corey (Tulane) CB	1997	**F**	
Draft, Chris (Stanford) LB	1998	Fada, Rob (Pittsburgh) G	1983–84
Dragos, Scott (Boston College) FB/TE	2000–01	Fain, Richard (Florida) CB	1992
Dreher, Ferd (Denver) E	1938	Falkenberg, Herb (Trinity) FB	1952
Dressen, Charley (no college) QB	1920	Famiglietti, Gary (Boston University) FB	1938–45
Drews, Ted (Princeton) E	1928	Fanning, Stan (Idaho) T	1960–62
Dreyer, Wally (Wisconsin) HB	1949	Farmer, George (UCLA) WR	1970–75
Driscoll, Paddy (Northwestern) HB	1920, 1926–29	Farrington, John (Prairie View) E	1960–63
Drulis, Chuck (Temple) G	1942, 1945–50	Farris, Tom (Wisconsin) QB	1946–47
Drury, Lyle (St. Louis) E	1930–31	Feathers, Beattie (Tennessee) HB	1934–37
Drzewiecki, Ron (Marquette) HB	1955, 1957	Febel, Fritz (Purdue) G	1935
Duarte, George (N. Arizona) CB	1987	Federovich, John (Davis & Elkins) T	1941–42
Duerson, Dave (Notre Dame) S	1983–89	Feichtinger, Andy (no college) E	1920–21
Dugger, Jack (Ohio State) E	1949	Fencik, Gary (Yale) S	1976–87
Dulaney, Mike (North Carolina) RB	1995–97	Fenimore, Bob (Oklahoma A&M) HB	1947
Dunlap, Bob (Oklahoma) QB	1935	Ferguson, J. B. (no college) T	1932
Dunsmore, Pat (Drake) TE	1983–84	Ferguson, Jim (South Carolina) C/LB	1969
Dyko, Chris (Washington State) T	1989	Fetz, Gus (no college) FB	1923
E		Figner, George (Colorado) HB	1953
Earl, Robin (Washington) RB–TE	1977–82	Finzer, Dave (DePauw) P	1984
Ecker, Ed (John Carroll) T	1947	Fisher, Bob (SMU) TE	1980–81
Edinger, Paul (Michigan State) K	2000–04	Fisher, Jeff (USC) CB	1981–84
Edwards, Cid (Tennessee State) RB	1975	Fitzgerald, Greg (Iowa) DT	1987
Edwards, Steve (Central Florida) T	2002–05	Flaherty, Pat (Princeton) E	1923
Eilers, Pat (Notre Dame) S	1995	Flanagan, Dick (Ohio State) G	1948–49
Elimimian, Abraham (Hawaii) DB	2005	Flanagan, Latham (Carnegie Tech) E	1931
Elliott, Jamin (Delaware) WR	2002	Flanigan, Jim (Notre Dame) DT	1994–2000
Ellis, Allan (UCLA) CB	1973–77, 1979–80	Fleckenstein, Bill (Iowa) G	1925–30
Elnes, Leland (Bradley) QB	1929	Floyd, Bobby Jack (TCU) FB	1953
Ely, Harold (Iowa) G	1932	Flutie, Doug (Boston College) QB	1986
Ely, Larry (Iowa) LB	1975	Fontenot, Al (Baylor) DE	1993–96
Engebretsen, Paul (Northwestern) G	1932	Fontenot, Jerry (Texas A&M) G	1989–96
Englund, Harry (no college) E	1920–23	Forbes, Marlon (Penn State) S	1996–98
Engram, Bobby (Penn State) WR	1996–2000	Ford, Charlie (Houston) CB	1971–73

Fordham, Jim (Georgia) FB	1944–45
Fordyce, Matt (Fordham) P	2005
Forrest, Tom (Cincinnati) G	1974
Forsey, Brock (Boise State) RB	2003
Forte, Aldo (Montana State) G	1939–42
Fortmann, Dan (Colgate) G	1936–43
Fortunato, Joe (Mississippi State) LB	1955–66
Francis, Sam (Nebraska) FB	1937–38
Franklin, Paul (Franklin) E	1930–34
Frazier, Leslie (Alcorn State) CB	1981–85
Frederick, Andy (New Mexico) T	1983–85
Friedman, Lennie (Duke) G	2005
Frump, Milton (Ohio Wesleyan) G	1930
Fuller, Steve (Clemson) QB	1984–86
Furrer, Will (Virginia Tech) QB	1992

G

Gage, Justin (Missouri) WR	2003–05
Gagnon, Dave (Ferris State) RB	1974
Gaines, Wentford (Cincinnati) CB	1978–80
Galimore, Willie (Florida A&M) HB	1957–63
Gallagher, Dave (Michigan) DE	1974
Gallarneau, Hugh (Stanford) HB	1941–42, 1945–47
Gandy, Mike (Notre Dame) G	2002–04
Garay, Antonio (Boston College) DT	2005
Gardocki, Chris (Clemson) P/K	1991–94
Garrett, Carl (New Mexico Highlands) RB	1973–74
Garrett, T. (Oklahoma A&M) C	1947–48
Garrett, W. D. (Mississippi State) T	1950
Garvey, A. "Hec" (Notre Dame) E	1922–25
Garvey, Ed (Notre Dame) HB	1925
Garza, Roberto (Texas A&M–Kingsville) C	2005
Gault, Willie (Tennessee) WR	1983–87
Gayle, Shaun (Ohio State) S	1984–94
Gedney, Chris (Syracuse) TE	1993–96
Gentry, Curtiss (Maryland State) DB	1966–68
Gentry, Dennis (Baylor) WR	1982–92
George, Bill (Wake Forest) G/LB	1952–65
Gepford, Sid (Millikin & Bethany) B	1920
Gersbach, Carl (West Chester State) LB	1975
Geyer, Bill (Colgate) HB	1942–43, 1946
Gibron, Abe (Purdue) G	1958–59

Gibson, Aaron (Wisconsin) T	2003–04
Gilbert, Kline (Mississippi) T	1953–57
Gilliam, John (South Carolina St.) WR	1977
Gilmore, John (Penn State) TE	2002–05
Glasgow, Brian (N. Illinois) TE	1987
Glenn, Bill (E. Illinois) QB	1944
Glueck, Larry (Villanova) B	1963–65
Goebel, Paul (Michigan) E	1925
Goodnight, Owen (Hardin–Sims) QB	1946
Gordon, Dick (Michigan State) WR	1965–71
Gordon, Lou (Illinois) T	1938
Gorgal, Ken (Purdue) HB	1955–56
Gould, Robbie (Penn State) K	2005
Gowins, Brian (Northwestern) K	1999
Grabowski, Jim (Illinois) RB	1971
Graham, Conrad (Tennessee) DB	1973
Graham, Jeff (Ohio State) WR	1994–95
Grandberry, Ken (Washington State) RB	1974
Grange, Garland "Gardie" (Illinois) E	1929–31
Grange, Harold "Red" (Illinois) HB	1925, 1929–34
Grant, Ernest (Arkansas–Pine Bluff) DT	2002
Grasmanis, Paul (Notre Dame) DT	1996–98
Gray, Bobby (Louisiana Tech) S	2002–05
Gray, Chris (Auburn) G	1997
Green, Bobby Joe (Florida) P	1962–73
Green, Jamaal (Miami) DE	2005
Green, Mark (Notre Dame) RB	1989–92
Green, Mike (Northwestern State) S	2000–05
Green, Robert (William & Mary) RB	1993–96
Greenwood, Glen (Iowa) HB	1924
Grim, Bob (Oregon State) WR	1975
Grossman, Rex (Florida) QB	2003–05
Grosvenor, George (Colorado) HB	1935–36
Grygo, Al (South Carolina) HB	1944–45
Gudauskas, Pete (Murray State) G	1943–44
Gulyanics, George (Ellisville JC) HB	1947–55
Gunn, Jimmy (USC) LB	1970–75
Gunner, Harry (Oregon State) DE	1970

H

Haddon, Aldous (Washington & Jefferson) B	1928
Haines, Kris (Notre Dame) WR	1979–81

Name	Years	Name	Years
Halas, George (Illinois) E	1920–29	Haynes, Michael (Penn State) DE	2003–05
Hale, Dave (Ottawa) DE	1969–71	Hazelton, Major (Florida A&M) DB	1968–69
Hall, Lemanski (Alabama) LB	1998	Healey, Ed (Dartmouth) T	1922–27
Hallock, Ty (Michigan State) FB	1998–99	Healy, Don (Maryland) G	1958–59
Haluska, Jim (Wisconsin) HB	1956	Hearden, Tom (Notre Dame) QB	1929
Hamity, Lewis (Chicago) HB	1941	Heck, Andy (Notre Dame) T	1994–98
Hamlin, Gene (Western Michigan) C	1971	Heileman, Charles (Iowa State) E	1939
Hammond, Henry (Southwestern) E	1937	Heimuli, Lakei (BYU) RB	1987
Hampton, Dan (Arkansas) DE	1979–90	Helwig, John (Notre Dame) G	1953–56
Hanke, Carl (Minnesota) G	1922	Hempel, Bill (Carroll) T	1942
Hanny, Frank (Indiana) E	1922–26	Henderson, Reuben (San Diego State) CB	1981–82
Hansen, Clifford (Luther) HB	1933	Hensley, Dick (Kentucky) E	1953
Hansen, Wayne (Texas Western) C	1950–59	Herndon, Jimmy (Houston) T	1997–2001
Harbaugh, Jim (Michigan) QB	1987–93	Herron, Bruce (New Mexico) LB	1978–82
Hardy, Cliff (Michigan State) CB	1971	Hester, Jim (North Dakota) TE	1970
Hardy, John (California) DB	1991	Hewitt, Bill (Michigan) E	1932–36
Harley, Charles "Chic" (Ohio State) RB	1921	Heyward, Craig (Pittsburgh) FB	1993
Harmon, Ronnie (Iowa) RB	1997	Hibbs, Jesse (USC) T	1931
Harper, LaSalle (Arkansas) LB	1989	Hicks, Michael (S. Carolina State) RB	1996–97
Harper, Roland (Louisiana Tech) RB	1975–78, 1980–82	Hicks, Tom (Illinois) LB	1976–80
		High, Lennie (no college) HB	1920
Harrell, Reggie (Texas Christian) WR	2005	Hiles, Van (Kentucky) S	1997
Harris, Al (Arizona State) DE	1979–84, 1986–87	Hilgenberg, Jay (Iowa) C	1981–91
		Hill, Harlon (Florence State Teachers) E	1954–61
Harris, Chris (Louisiana–Monroe) FS	2005	Hill, Ike (Catawba) WR	1973–74
Harris, Chuck (West Virginia) T	1987	Hillenmeyer, Hunter (Vanderbilt) LB	2003–05
Harris, Frank (NC State) RB	1987	Hilliard, Randy (NW Louisiana) CB	1998
Harris, Raymont (Ohio State) RB	1994–97	Hintz, Mike (Wisconsin–Platteville) DB	1987
Harris, Richard (Grambling) DE	1974–75	Hoban, Mike (Michigan) G	1974
Harris, Sean (Arizona) LB	1995–2000	Hobscheid, Fred (Chicago) G	1927
Harris, Tommie (Oklahoma) DT	2004–05	Hodgins, Norm (LSU) S	1974
Harris, Walt (Mississippi State) CB	1996–2001	Hoffman, Jack (Xavier) E	1952–56
Harris, Willie (Mississippi State) WR	1993	Hoffman, John (Hawaii) DE	1971
Harrison, Jim (Missouri) RB	1971–74	Hoffman, John (Arkansas) E	1949–56
Hart, Tommy (Morris Brown) DE	1978–79	Hoge, Merril (Idaho) RB	1994
Hartenstine, Mike (Penn State) DE	1975–86	Hohensee, Mike (Minnesota) QB	1987
Hartman, Fred (Rice) T	1947	Hoke, Jonathan (Ball State) CB	1980
Hartnett, Perry (SMU) G	1982–83	Holdman, Warrick (Texas A&M) LB	1999–2002
Hartsell, Mark (Boston College) QB	2000	Holloway, Glen (N. Texas State) G	1970–73
Haselrig, Clint (Michigan) WR	1974	Hollowell, T.J. (Nebraska) LB	2005
Hatley, John (Sul Ross) G	1953	Holly, Daven (Cincinnati) CB	2005
Hawkins, Garland (Syracuse) DE	1995	Holman, Willie (South Carolina State) DE	1968–73

Holmer, Walter (Northwestern) FB	1929–30	Jackson, Noah (Tampa) G	1975–83
Holmes, Jaret (Auburn) K	1999	Jackson, Randy (Florida) T	1967–74
Holovak, Mike (Boston College) FB	1947–48	Jackson, Vestee (Washington) CB	1986–90
Hoptowit, Al (Washington State) T	1941–45	Jaeger, Jeff (Washington) K	1996–99
Horan, Mike (Long Beach State) P	1998	Jagade, Chick (Indiana) FB	1954–55
Horton, Larry (Iowa) DT	1972–73	James, Dan (Ohio State) T	1967
Howard, Bobbie (Notre Dame) LB	2001–03	Janata, John (Illinois) T	1983
Howard, Dana (Illinois) LB	1996	Janet, Ernie (Washington) G	1972–74
Howley, Charles (West Virginia) C	1958–59	January, Mike (Texas) LB	1987
Hrivnak, Gary (Purdue) DT	1973–76	Jarmoluk, Mike (Temple) T	1946–47
Huarte, John (Notre Dame) QB	1972	Jecha, Ralph (Northwestern) G	1955
Hudson, Chris (Colorado) S	1999	Jeffries, Eric (Texas) CB	1987
Huerta, Carlos (Miami–FL) K	1996	Jencks, Robert (Miami, OH) E	1963–64
Huff, Gary (Florida State) QB	1973–76	Jenkins, Corey (South Carolina) LB	2004
Huffine, Ken (Purdue) FB	1921	Jennings, Keith (Clemson) TE	1991–97
Hugasian, Harry (Stanford) HB	1955	Jensvold, Leo (Iowa) QB	1931
Hughes, Billy (Texas) C	1940–41	Jeter, Bob (Iowa) CB	1971–73
Hughes, Tyrone (Nebraska) PR/KR	1997	Jeter, Perry (California Poly Tech) RB	1956–57
Hull, Mike (USC) FB	1968–70	Jewett, Bob (Michigan State) E	1958
Hultz, Don (Southern Mississippi) DT	1974	Jiggetts, Dan (Harvard) T	1976–82
Humphries, Stefan (Michigan) G	1984–86	Joe, Leon (Maryland) LB	2004–05
Hunsinger, Chuck (Florida) HB	1950–52	Joesting, Herb (Minnesota) FB	1931–32
Hunt, Jackie (Marshall) HB	1945	Johnson, Albert (Kentucky) FB	1938
Huntington, Greg (Penn State) G	1997–99	Johnson, Anthony (Notre Dame) RB	1995
Hurst, William (Oregon) G	1924	Johnson, Bill (SMU) G	1946–47
Hutchinson, Chad (Stanford) QB	2004	Johnson, Bryan (Boise State) FB	2004–05
Hutchison, Anthony (Texas Tech) RB	1983–84	Johnson, Greg (Florida State) DT	1977
Huther, Bruce (New Hampshire) LB	1982	Johnson, Jack (Miami) B	1957–59
Hyche, Steve (Livingston) LB	1989	Johnson, John (Indiana) T	1963–68
Hyland, Bob (Boston College) C	1970	Johnson, Keshon (Arizona) CB	1993–95
		Johnson, Leo (Millikin) HB	1920
I		Johnson, Leon (North Carolina) RB	2001–02
Idonije, Israel (Manitoba, Canada) DE	2004–05	Johnson, O. G. (no college) FB	1924
Ingwersen, Burt (Illinois) G	1920–21	Johnson, Pete (VMI) B	1959
Ippolito, Anthony (Purdue) G	1943	Johnson, Robert (Auburn) TE	2003
Ireland, Darwin (Arkansas) LB	1994–95	Johnson, Tank (Washington) DT	2004–05
Ivlow, John (Colorado State) RB	1993	Johnson, Todd (Florida) S	2004–05
		Johnson, Troy (Oklahoma) LB	1988–89
J		Johnson, Will (NE Louisiana) LB	1987
Jackson, Bobby (Alabama) HB	1961	Johnsos, Luke (Northwestern) E	1929–37
Jackson, Jack (Florida) WR	1995–96	Jones, Bob (San Diego State) E	1967
Jackson, John (USC) WR	1996	Jones, Dante (Oklahoma) LB	1988–94

Jones, Daryl (Miami) WR — 2004
Jones, Edgar (Pittsburgh) HB — 1945
Jones, Greg (Colorado) LB — 2001
Jones, Jermaine (Northwestern State) CB — 1999
Jones, Jerry (Notre Dame) G — 1920–21
Jones, Jimmy (Wisconsin) E — 1965–67
Jones, Stan (Maryland) T — 1954–65
Jones, Thomas (Virginia) RB — 2004–05
Jordan, Donald (Houston) RB — 1984
Joseph, Dwayne (Syracuse) CB — 1995–96
Joyce, Eric (Tennessee State) CB — 2002
Juenger, Dave (Ohio U.) WR — 1973
Jurkovic, Mirko (Notre Dame) G — 1992

K

Karr, William (West Virginia) E — 1933–38
Karras, Ted (Indiana) G — 1960–64
Karwales, Jack (Michigan) E — 1946–47
Kashama, Alain (Michigan) DE — 2004
Kassel, Chuck (Illinois) E — 1927
Kavanaugh, Ken (LSU) E — 1940–41, 1945–50
Kawal, Ed (Illinois) C — 1931–36
Keane, Jim (Iowa State) E — 1946–51
Keefe, Jerry (Notre Dame) G — 1920
Kelly, Elmo (Wichita U.) E — 1944
Kelly, Jim (Tennessee State) TE — 1974
Kendricks, Jim (Texas A&M) T — 1924
Kennison, Eddie (LSU) WR — 2000
Keriasotis, Nick (St. Ambrose) G — 1942–44
Keyes, Marcus (North Alabama) DT — 1996–97
Keys, Tyrone (Mississippi St.) DE — 1983–85
Kiesling, Walter (St. Thomas) G — 1934
Kilcullen, Bob (Texas Tech) T — 1957–65
Kilgore, Jon (Auburn) P — 1968
Kindt, Don (Wisconsin) HB — 1947–55
Kindt, Don Jr. (Wisconsin–LaCrosse) TE — 1987
King, Ralph (Chicago) T — 1925
Kinney, Steve (Utah State) T — 1973–74
Kirk, Ken (Mississippi) C — 1960
Kissell, Adolph (Boston College) FB — 1942
Klawitter, Dick (S. Dakota State) C — 1956–57

Klein, Dick (Iowa) T — 1958–59
Knapczyk, Ken (Northern Iowa) WR — 1987
Knight, Bryan (Pittsburgh) LB — 2002–03
Knop, Oscar (Illinois) FB — 1923–28
Knox, Bill (Purdue) DB — 1974–76
Knox, Ron (UCLA) QB — 1957
Koehler, Robert (Northwestern) FB — 1920–21
Kolman, Ed (Temple) T — 1940–44
Konovsky, Bob (Wisconsin) G — 1960
Kopcha, Joe (Chattanooga) G — 1929–35
Kortas, Kenneth (Louisville) T — 1969
Kosins, Gary (Dayton) RB — 1972–74
Kozlowski, Glen (BYU) WR — 1987–92
Kramer, Erik (NC State) QB — 1994–98
Kreamcheck, John (William & Mary) T — 1953–55
Kreitling, Rich (Illinois) E — 1964
Kreiwald, Doug (West Texas State) G — 1967–68
Krenk, Mitch (Nebraska) TE — 1984
Krenzel, Craig (Ohio State) QB — 2004
Kreutz, Olin (Washington) C — 1998–2005
Krieg, Dave (Milton College –WI) QB — 1996
Krumm, Todd (Michigan State) S — 1988
Kuechenberg, Rudy (Indiana) LB — 1967–69
Kunz, Lee (Nebraska) LB — 1979–81
Kurek, Ralph (Wisconsin) FB — 1965–70

L

Lacina, Corbin (Augustana, SD) C — 2003
LaFavor, Tron (Florida) DT — 2003
LaFleur, Joe (Marquette) FB — 1922–24
LaForest, W. (no college) FB — 1920
Lahar, Harold (Oklahoma) G — 1941, 1945
Lamb, Walter (Oklahoma) E — 1946
Landry, Greg (Massachusetts) QB — 1984
Lanum, R. "Jake" (Illinois & Millikin) QB — 1920–24
Larsen, Stephen (San Diego State) LB — 2005
Larson, Fred (Notre Dame) C — 1922
Lashar, Tim (Oklahoma) K — 1987
Lasker, Greg (Arkansas) S — 1988
Latta, Greg (Morgan State) TE — 1975–80
Lawler, Allen (Texas) HB — 1948
Lawson, Roger (W. Michigan) RB — 1972–73

Layne, Bobby (Texas) QB	1948
Leahy, Bernie (Notre Dame) HB	1932
Leclerc, Roger (Trinity) K/LB	1960–66
Lee, Buddy (LSU) QB	1971
Lee, Herman (Florida A&M) T	1958–66
Lee, Shawn (North Alabama) DE	1998
Leeuwenburg, Jay (Colorado) G	1992–95
Leeuwenburg, Rich (Stanford) T	1965
Leggett, Earl (LSU) T	1957–65
Lemon, Clifford (Centre) T	1926
Leonard, James (Colgate) T	1924
Lesane, James (Virginia) HB	1952–53
Lewis, Darren (Texas A&M) RB	1991–93
Lewis, Nate (Oregon Tech) WR	1994–95
Lewis, Scotty (Baylor) DT	1995
Lick, Dennis (Wisconsin) T	1976–81
Lincoln, Jeremy (Tennessee) CB	1992–95
Line, Bill (SMU) DT	1972
Lintzenich, Joseph (St. Louis) FB	1930–31
Lipscomb, Paul (Tennessee) T	1954
Lisch, Rusty (Notre Dame) QB	1984
Littleton, Jody (Baylor) C	2002
Livers, Virgil (W. Kentucky) CB	1975–79
Livingston, Andy (Phoenix JC) B	1964–65
Livingston, Howie (Fullerton JC) DB	1953
Logan, James (Indiana) G	1942–43
Long, Harvey (Detroit) T	1929
Long, Johnny (Colgate) QB	1944–45
Long, Khari (Baylor) DE	2005
Lowe, Lloyd (North Texas State) HB	1953–54
Lowery, Michael (Mississippi) LB	1996–97
Luckman, Sid (Columbia) QB	1939–50
Lujack, Johnny (Notre Dame) QB	1948–51
Lundy, Dennis (Northwestern) RB	1995
Lusby, Vaughn (Arkansas) CB	1980
Lyle, Garry (G. Washington) CB	1968–74
Lyman, Dustin (Wake Forest) TE	2000–04
Lyman, Roy "Link" (Nebraska) T	1926–28, 1930–31, 1933–34
Lynch, Lorenzo (Cal State–Sacramento) DB	1987–89
Lyon, George (Kansas State) T	1929

M

MacLeod, Robert (Dartmouth) HB	1939–40
Macon, Ed (College of Pacific) HB	1952–53
MacWherter, Kile (Bethany) FB	1920
Magnani, Dante (St. Mary's) HB	1943, 1946, 1949
Maillard, Ralph (Creighton) T	1929
Malone, Charles (Texas A&M) E	1933
Manders, Jack (Minnesota) HB	1933–40
Maness, James (TCU) WR	1985
Mangum, John (Alabama) S	1990–98
Maniaci, Joe (Fordham) RB	1938–41
Mannelly, Patrick (Duke) T/LS	1998–2005
Manning, Pete (Wake Forest) E	1960–61
Manske, Edgar (Northwestern) E	1937–40
Marconi, Joe (West Virginia) FB	1962–66
Margarita, Bob (Brown) HB	1944–46
Margerum, Ken (Stanford) WR	1981–83, 1985–86
Marshall, Alfonso (Miami) CB	2004–05
Marshall, Anthony (LSU) DB	1994–97
Marshall, Wilber (Florida) LB	1984–87
Martin, Bill (Georgia Tech) E	1964–65
Martin, Billy (Minnesota) HB	1962–64
Martin, Chris (Northwestern) CB	1996
Martin, Dave (Notre Dame) LB	1969
Martin, Frank (Alabama) HB	1941
Martinovich, P. (College of Pacific) G	1940
Maslowski, Matt (San Diego University) WR	1972
Mass, Wayne (Clemson) OT	1968–70
Masters, Bob (Baylor) FB	1943–44
Masterson, Bernie (Nebraska) QB	1934–40
Masterson, Forest (Iowa) C	1945
Mastrogany, Gus (Iowa) E	1931
Matheson, Jack (W. Michigan) E	1947
Mattes, Ron (Virginia) T	1991
Matthews, Shane (Florida) QB	1993–96, 1999–2001
Mattson, Riley (Oregon) T	1965
Matuza, Al (Georgetown) C	1941–44
Maumalanga, Chris (Kansas) DT	1997
May, Chester (no college) G	1920
May, Walter O. "Red" (no college) G	1920
Mayes, Alonzo (Oklahoma State) TE	1998–2000
Mayes, Rufus (Ohio State) T	1969

Maynard, Brad (Ball State) P	2001–05	Michaels, Edward (Villanova) G	1935
Maznicki, F. (Boston College) HB	1942–43	Mihal, Joe (Purdue) T	1940–41
McAfee, George (Duke) HB	1940–41, 1945–50	Milburn, Glyn (Stanford) RB/KR	1998–2001
McClendon, Willie (Georgia) RB	1979–82	Miller, Charles "Ookie" (Purdue) C	1932–37
McColl, Bill (Stanford) E	1952–59	Miller, Fred (Baylor) T	2005
McCray, Bruce (W. Illinois) CB	1987	Miller, Jim (Michigan State) QB	1998–2000, 2002
McDonald, Lester (Nebraska) E	1937–39	Miller, Milford (Chadron) T	1932
McDonald, Rico (Pitt) LB	1998–99	Milner, Bill (Duke) G	1947–49
McElroy, Ray (Eastern Illinois) S	2000	Milton, Eldridge (Clemson) LB	1987
McElwain, Bill (Northwestern) HB	1925	Miniefield, Kevin (Arizona State) CB	1993–96
McEnulty, Doug (Wichita) FB	1943–44	Minini, Frank (San Jose State) HB	1947–49
McGee, Tony (Bishop College) DE	1971–73	Minter, Barry (Tulsa) LB	1993–2000
McGowan, Brandon (Maine) SS	2005	Mintun, John F. "Jack" (no college) C	1921–22
McGuire, Gene (Notre Dame) C	1993	Mirer, Rick (Notre Dame) QB	1997
McInerney, Sean (Frostburg State) DT	1987	Mitchell, Charley (Tulsa) HB	1945
McKenzie, Keith (Ball State) DE	2002	Mitchell, Qasim (North Carolina A&T) G	2004–05
McKie, Jason (Temple) FB	2003–05	Mohardt, John (Notre Dame) HB	1925
McKinnely, Phil (UCLA) T	1982	Molesworth, Keith (Monmouth) HB	1931–37
McKinney, Bill (West Texas) LB	1972	Montgomery, Randy (Weber State) CB	1974
McKinnon, Dennis (Florida State) WR	1983–85, 1987–89	Montgomery, Ross (TCU) FB	1969–70
		Mooney, Jim (Georgetown) E	1935
McLean, Ray (St. Anselm) HB	1940–47	Mooney, Tip (Abilene Christian) HB	1944–46
McMahon, Jim (BYU) QB	1982–88	Moore, Albert (Northwestern) QB	1932
McMichael, Steve (Texas) DT	1981–93	Moore, Damon (Ohio State) DB	2002
McMillen, Jim (Illinois) G	1924–29	Moore, Jerry (Arkansas) S	1971–72
McMillon, Todd (N. Arizona) CB	2000–04	Moore, Joe (Missouri) RB	1971–72
McMullen, Daniel (Nebraska) G	1930–31	Moore, McNeil (Sam Houston) HB	1954–56
McMurtry, Greg (Michigan) WR	1994	Moore, Rocco (Western Michigan) G	1980
McNown, Cade (UCLA) QB	1999–2000	Moorehead, Emery (Colorado) TE	1981–88
McPherson, Forrest (Nebraska) G	1935	Moreno, Moses (Colorado State) QB	1998
McQuarters, R.W. (Oklahoma State) CB	2000–04	Morgan, Anthony (Tennessee) WR	1991–93
McRae, Bennie (Michigan) HB	1962–70	Morgan, Mike (Wisconsin) RB	1978
McRae, Franklin (Tennessee State) DT	1967	Morris, Byron "Bam" (Texas Tech) RB	1998
Meadows, Ed (Duke) E	1954–56	Morris, Francis (Boston University) HB	1942
Mellekas, John (Arizona) T	1956–61	Morris, Johnny (Santa Barbara) FL	1958–67
Merkel, Monte (Kansas) G	1942–43	Morris, Jon (Holy Cross) C	1978
Merrill, Mark (Minnesota) LB	1979	Morris, Larry (Georgia Tech) LB	1959–65
Merrill, Than (Yale) S	2001	Morris, Ray (UTEP) LB	1987
Merritt, Ahmad (Wisconsin) WR	2001–03	Morris, Ron (SMU) WR	1987–92
Metcalf, Terrence (Mississippi) G	2002–05	Morrison, Fred (Ohio State) FB	1950–53
Meyers, Denny (Iowa) T	1931	Morrissey, Jim (Michigan State) LB	1985–93
Meyers, Jerry (N. Illinois) DL	1976–79	Morton, John (Missouri) HB	1945

Moser, Robert (Pacific) C	1951–53	Norris, Jon (American International) DE	1987
Mosley, Anthony (Fresno State) RB	1987	Norvell, Jay (Iowa) LB	1987
Mosley, Henry (Morris Brown) HB	1955	Novoselsky, Brent (Penn) TE	1988
Mucha, Charles (Washington) G	1935	Nowaskey, Bob (George Washington) E	1940–42
Mucha, Rudy (Washington) G	1945–46		
Muckensturm, Jerry (Arkansas State) LB	1976–82	**O**	
Mudd, Howard (Hillsdale) G	1969–70	O'Bradovich, Ed (Illinois) DE	1962–71
Muhammad, Muhsin (Michigan State) WR	2005	O'Connell, J. F. (Penn State) C	1924
Mullen, Vern (Illinois) E	1923–25	O'Connell, Tom (Illinois) QB	1953
Mullins, Don R. (Houston) HB	1961–62	O'Neill, Pat (Syracuse) P	1995
Mullins, Noah (Kentucky) HB	1946–49	O'Quinn, John (Wake Forest) E	1950–51
Mundee, Fred (Notre Dame) C	1943–45	O'Rourke, Charles (Boston College) QB	1942
Murray, Richard (Marquette) T	1924	Oakley, Anthony (Western Kentucky) G	2005
Murry, Don (Wisconsin) T	1924–31	Obee, Terry (Oregon) WR	1993–94
Musso, George (Millikin) G	1933–44	Odom, Joe (Purdue) LB	2003–05
Musso, Johnny (Alabama) RB	1975–77	Oech, Verne (Minnesota) G	1936
Muster, Brad (Stanford) FB	1988–92	Oelerich, John (St. Ambrose) HB	1938
Myslinski, Tom (Tennessee) OL	1993–94	Ogden, Ray (Alabama) TE	1969–71
		Ogunleye, Adewale (Indiana) DE	2004
N		Oliver, Jack (Memphis State) T	1987
Nagurski, Bronko (Minnesota) FB	1930–37, 1943	Ortego, Keith (McNeese State) WR	1985–87
Neacy, Clement (Colgate) E	1927	Orton, Kyle (Purdue) QB	2005
Neal, Dan (Kentucky) C	1975–83	Osborne, Jim (Southern) DT	1972–84
Neal, Ed (LSU) G	1951	Osmanski, Bill (Holy Cross) FB	1939–43, 1946–47
Neck, Tommy (LSU) HB	1962	Osmanski, Joe (Holy Cross) FB	1946–49
Neely, Bobby (Virginia) TE	1996	Owens, John (Notre Dame) TE	2004
Negus, Fred (Wisconsin) C	1950		
Neidert, John (Louisville) LB	1970	**P**	
Nelson, Everett (Illinois) T	1929	Pagac, Fred (Ohio State) TE	1974
Nesbitt, Dick (Drake) HB	1930–33	Page, Alan (Notre Dame) DT	1978–81
Newkirk, Robert (Michigan State) DT	2000–01	Parrish, Tony (Washington) S	1998–2001
Newsome, Billy (Grambling) DE	1977	Parsons, Bob (Penn State) P-TE	1972–81
Newton, Bob (Nebraska) G	1971–75	Patterson, Billy (Baylor) QB	1939
Nickla, Ed (Maryland) G	1959	Paul, Markus (Syracuse) S	1989–92
Nielsen, Hans (Michigan State) K	1981	Pauley, Frank Don (Washington & Jefferson) T	1930
Nix, Kent (TCU) QB	1970–71	Payton, Sean (E. Illinois) QB	1987
Nolting, Ray (Cincinnati) HB	1936–43	Payton, Walter (Jackson State) RB	1975–87
Norberg, Hank (Stanford) E	1948	Pearce, W. "Pard" (Penn) QB	1920–22
Nordquist, Mark (Pacific) G/C	1975–76	Pearson, Madison (Kansas) C	1929–34
Nori, Reino (DeKalb) HB	1938	Pederson, Jim (Augsburg) HB	1932
Norman, Dick (Stanford) QB	1961	Peiffer, Dan (SE Missouri State) C	1975–77
Norman, Tim (Illinois) G	1983	Percival, Mac (Texas Tech) K	1967–73

Perez, Peter (Illinois) G	1945	Pruitt, Mickey (Colorado) LB	1988–90
Perina, Bob (Princeton) HB	1949–50	Purnell, James (Wisconsin) LB	1964–68
Perini, Pete (Ohio State) FB	1954–55	Pyle, Mike (Yale) C	1961–69
Perkins, Don (Plattesville) FB	1945–46		
Perrin, Lonnie (Illinois) RB	1979	**Q**	
Perry, Todd (Kentucky) G	1993–2000	Quinn, Jonathan (Middle Tennessee State) QB	2004
Perry, William (Clemson) DT	1985–93		
Peter, Christian (Nebraska) DT	2002	**R**	
Peterson, Adrian (Georgia Southern) RB	2002–05	Rabold, Mike (Indiana) G	1964–67
Peterson, Anthony (Notre Dame) LB	1997	Rains, Dan (Cincinnati) LB	1982–85
Petitbon, Richie (Tulane) HB	1959–68	Rakestraw, Larry (Georgia) QB	1964–67
Petty, John (Purdue) FB	1942	Ramsey, Frank (Oregon State) G	1945
Petty, Ross (Illinois) G	1920	Rather, Bo (Michigan) WR	1974–78
Phillips, Loyd (Arkansas) DE	1967–69	Reader, Russ (Michigan State) HB	1947
Phillips, Reggie (SMU) CB	1985–87	Reese, Lloyd (Tennessee) FB	1946
Phipps, Mike (Purdue) QB	1977–81	Reese, Marcus (UCLA) LB	2004–05
Piccolo, Brian (Wake Forest) RB	1966–69	Reeves, Carl (North Carolina State) DE	1996–98
Pickens, Bob (Nebraska) T	1967–68	Reid, Gabe (Brigham Young) TE	2003, 2005
Pickering, Clay (Maine) WR	1986	Reilly, Mike (Iowa) LB	1964–68
Pierson, Shurron (South Florida) DE	2004	Rentie, Caesar (Oklahoma) T	1988
Pifferini, Bob (UCLA) LB	1972–75	Rentner, Ernest "Pug" (Northwestern) HB	1936–37
Pilgrim, Evan (BYU) G	1995–97	Reppond, Mike (Arkansas) WR	1973
Pinder, Cyril (Illinois) RB	1971–72	Reynolds, Tom (San Diego State) WR	1973
Pippins, Jerrell (Nebraska) S	2004	Rice, Andy (Texas Southern) DT	1972–73
Plank, Doug (Ohio State) S	1975–82	Richards, Golden (Hawaii) WR	1978–79
Plasman, Dick (Vanderbilt) E	1937–41, 1944	Richards, Ray (Nebraska) T	1933–36
Podmajersky, Paul (Illinois) G	1944	Richardson, Mike (Arizona State) CB	1983–88
Polisky, John (Notre Dame) G	1929	Richman, Harry (Illinois) G	1929
Polk, Octus (Stephen F. Austin) G	1995–96	Riley, Karon (Minnesota) DE/LB	2001
Pollock, Bill (Pennsylvania Military Academy) HB	1935–36	Riley, Pat (Miami–FL) DT	1995
Pool, Hampton (Stanford) E	1940–43	Rivera, Ron (California) LB	1984–92
Potter, Kevin (Missouri) S	1983–84	Rivera, Steve (California) WR	1977
Powell, Carl (Louisville) DE	2001	Rivers, Garland (Michigan) DB	1987
President, Andre (Angelo State) TE	1995	Rives, Don (Texas Tech) LB	1973–78
Preston, Pat (Wake Forest) G	1946–49	Roberts, Tom (DePaul) G	1943–44
Price, Terry (Texas A&M) DT	1990	Roberts, Willie (Houston) CB	1973
Pride, Dan (Jackson State) LB	1968–69	Robertson, Bernard (Tulane) T	2002
Primus, Greg (Colorado State) WR	1994–95	Robinson, Bryan (Fresno State) DL	1998–2003
Pritchett, Stanley (South Carolina) FB	2001–03	Robinson, Marcus (S. Carolina) WR	1997–2001
Proctor, Rex (Rice) HB	1953	Rodenhauser, Mark (Illinois State) C	1987–88
		Roder, Mirro (no college) K	1973–74

Roehlk, Jon (Iowa) G	1987	Schreiber, Larry (Tennessee Tech) RB	1976
Roehnelt, William (Bradley) G	1958–59	Schroeder, Gene (Virginia) E	1951–52,
Rogers, Mel (Florida A&M) LB	1977		1954–57
Roggeman, Tom (Purdue) G	1956–57	Schubert, Steve (U. Mass.) WR	1975–79
Romanik, Steve (Villanova) QB	1950–53	Schuette, Paul (Wisconsin) G	1930–32
Romney, Milton (Chicago) QB	1925–29	Schultz, Bill (USC) G	1997
Ronzani, Gene (Marquette) QB	1933–38, 1944–45	Schwantz, Jim (Purdue) LB	1992, 1998
Roper, John (Texas A&M) LB	1989–92	Schweda, Brian (Kansas) DE	1966
Rosequist, Ted (Ohio State) T	1934–36	Schweidler, Dick (St. Louis) HB	1938–39, 1946
Rothschild, Doug (Wheaton) LB	1987	Scott, Ian (Florida) DT	2003–05
Rouse, James (Arkansas) RB	1990–91	Scott, James (Henderson JC) WR	1976–80, 1982
Roveto, John (SW Louisiana) K	1981–82	Scott, Ralph (Wisconsin) T	1921–25
Rowden, Larry (Houston) LB	1971	Seals, George (Missouri) G	1965–71
Rowell, Eugene (Dubuque) DT	1987	Seibering, Gerald (Drake) FB	1932
Rowland, Brad (McMurry) HB	1951	Senn, Bill (Knox) HB	1926–31
Rowland, Justin (TCU) HB	1960	Serini, Washington (Kentucky) G	1948–51
Rubens, Larry (Montana State) C	1986	Setzer, Bobby (Boise State) DE	2002
Rupp, Nelson (Dennison) QB	1921	Sevy, Jeff (California) T/DE	1975–78
Russell, Reginald (Northwestern) E	1928	Seward, Len (E. Illinois) LS	1987
Ryan, John (Detroit) T	1929	Seymour, Jim (Notre Dame) WR	1970–72
Ryan, Rocky (Illinois) E	1958	Shank, J. L. (no college) HB	1920
Ryan, Tim (USC) DT	1990–93	Shanklin, Ron (N. Texas State) WR	1975–76
Rydalch, Ron (Utah) DT	1975–80	Shannon, John (Kentucky) DT	1988–89
Rydzewski, Frank (Notre Dame) C	1923	Shaw, Glenn (Kentucky) HB	1960
Rykovich, Julie (Illinois) HB	1949–51	Shearer, Brad (Texas) DT	1978–80
		Shedd, Kenny (Northern Iowa) WR	1994
S		Shellog, Alec (Notre Dame) T	1939
Sacrinty, Nick (Wake Forest) QB	1947	Shelton, Daimon (Sacramento State) FB	2001–02
Salaam, Rashaan (Colorado) RB	1995–97	Sherman, Saul (Chicago) QB	1939–40
Saldi, Jay (South Carolina) TE	1983–84	Shipkey, Jerry (UCLA) FB	1953
Samuel, Khari (Massachusetts) LB	1999–2001	Shivers, Jason (Arizona State) S	2004
Sanders, Glenell (Louisiana Tech) LB	1990	Shoemake, Hub (Illinois) G	1920–21
Sanders, Thomas (Texas A&M) RB	1985–89	Shy, Don (San Diego State) RB	1970–72
Sanderson, Reggie (Stanford) RB	1973	Siegal, John (Columbia) E	1939–43
Sanderson, Scott (Washington State) G	2003	Sigillo, Dom (Xavier) T	1943–44
Sauerbrun, Todd (West Virginia) P	1995–99	Sigmund, Arthur W. (no college) G	1923
Sauter, Cory (Minnesota) QB	2002	Simmons, Clyde (W. Carolina) DE	1999–2000
Savoldi, Joe (Notre Dame) FB	1930	Simmons, David (North Carolina) LB	1983
Sayers, Gale (Kansas) HB	1965–71	Simmons, J. (Bethune–Cookman) WR	1969
Schiechl, John (Santa Clara) C	1945–46	Simpson, Carl (Florida State) DT	1993–97
Schmidt, Terry (Ball State) S	1976–84	Sinceno, Kaseem (Syracuse) TE	2000

Singletary, Mike (Baylor) LB — 1981–92

Sisk, John (Marquette) HB — 1932–36

Sisk, John Jr. (Miami) B — 1964

Skibinski, John (Purdue) RB — 1978–81

Smeja, Rudy (Michigan) E — 1944–45

Smith, Clarence (Georgia) E — 1942

Smith, Eric (LSU) WR — 1997

Smith, Eugene (Georgia Tech) G — 1930

Smith, Frankie (Baylor) CB — 1998–2000

Smith, H. Allen (Mississippi) E — 1947–48

Smith, J. D. (N. Carolina A&T) FB — 1956

Smith, James (Compton JC) HB — 1961

Smith, Justin (Indiana) LB — 2005

Smith, Quintin (Kansas) WR — 1990

Smith, Ray Gene (Midwestern) HB — 1954–57

Smith, Ron (Wisconsin) S — 1965, 1970–72

Smith, Russell (Illinois) T — 1921–23

Smith, Sean (Grambling) DT — 1987–88

Smith, Thomas (North Carolina) CB — 2000

Smith, Vernice (Florida A&M) G — 1993

Smith, Vinson (East Carolina) LB — 1993–96

Snow, Percy (Michigan State) LB — 1993

Snyder, Bob (Ohio University) QB — 1939–41, 1943

Sorey, Revie (Illinois) G — 1975–82

Spears, Marcus (NW Louisiana State) T — 1994–96

Spellman, Alonzo (Ohio State) DL — 1992–97

Spero, Kenny (Morehead State) C — 1942

Spivey, Mike (Colorado) CB — 1977–79

Sprinkle, Ed (Hardin–Simmons) E — 1944–55

St. Clair, John (Virginia) T — 2005

Stachowicz, Ray (Michigan State) P — 1983

Stahlman, Dick (DePaul) T — 1933

Staley, Bill (Utah State) DT — 1970–71

Stamper, John (South Carolina) DE — 2002

Standlee, Norm (Stanford) FB — 1941

Stargell, Tony (Tennessee State) CB — 1997

Stautberg, Gerald (Cincinnati) G — 1951

Steinbach, Larry (St. Thomas) G — 1930–31

Steinkemper, Bill (Notre Dame) T — 1942–43

Stenn, Paul (Villanova) G — 1948–51

Stenstrom, Steve (Stanford) QB — 1995–98

Sternaman, Edward (Illinois) HB — 1920–30

Sternaman, Joe (Illinois) HB — 1922–29

Steuber, Bob (Missouri) HB — 1943

Stewart, Kordell (Colorado) QB — 2003

Stickel, Walt (Penn) T — 1946–49

Stillwell, Roger (Stanford) DE–DT — 1975–77

Stinchcomb, Pete (Ohio State) QB — 1921–22

Stinson, Lemuel (Texas Tech) CB — 1988–92

Stoepel, Terry (Tulsa) G — 1967

Stolfa, Anton (Luther) HB — 1939

Stone, Billy (Bradley) HB — 1951–54

Stonebreaker, Michael (Notre Dame) LB — 1991

Stoops, Mike (Iowa) DS — 1987

Streeter, George (Notre Dame) DB — 1989

Strickland, Larry (North Texas State) C — 1954–59

Sturtridge, Dick (DePaul) HB — 1928–29

Stydahar, Joe (West Virginia) T — 1936–42, 1945–46

Suhey, Matt (Penn State) RB — 1980–89

Sullivan, Frank (Loyola, NO) C — 1935–39

Sumner, Charles (William & Mary) HB — 1955, 1958–60

Sutherland, Vinnie (Purdue) WR — 2002

Sweeney, Jake (Cincinnati) T — 1944

Swisher, Bob (Northwestern) HB — 1938–41, 1945

Symons, B.J. (Texas Tech) QB — 2005

Szymanski, Frank (Notre Dame) C — 1949

T

Tabor, Paul (Oklahoma) C — 1980

Tackwell, C.O. (Kansas State) E — 1931–33

Tafoya, Joe (Arizona) DE — 2001–03

Taft, Merrill (Wisconsin) FB — 1924

Tait, John (Brigham Young) T — 2004–05

Tate, David (Colorado) S — 1988–92

Tate, Lars (Georgia) RB — 1990

Taylor, Brian (Oregon State) RB — 1989

Taylor, Clifton (Memphis State) RB — 1974

Taylor, Henry (South Carolina) DT — 2001

Taylor, Joe (N. Carolina A&T) DB — 1967–74

Taylor, J.R. "Tarz" (Ohio State) G — 1921–22

Taylor, Ken (Oregon St.) CB — 1985

Taylor, Lionel (NM Highland University) E — 1959

Taylor, Roosevelt (Grambling) DB — 1961–68

Teafatiller, Guy (Illinois) DL — 1987

Terrell, David (Michigan) WR	2001–04	Veach, Walter (no college) HB	1920
Thayer, Tom (Notre Dame) G	1985–92	Venturelli, Fred (no college) T	1948
Thierry, John (Alcorn State) DE	1994–98	Vick, Ernie (Michigan) C	1925–27
Thomas, Anthony (Michigan) RB	2001–04	Vick, Richard (Washington & Jefferson) QB	1925
Thomas, Bob (Notre Dame) K	1975–84	Villarrial, Chris (Indiana–PA) C	1996–2003
Thomas, Calvin (Illinois) FB	1982–87	Vodicka, Joe (Lewis Institute) HB	1943–45
Thomas, Earl (Houston) WR	1971–73	Voss, Walter "Tillie" (Detroit) E	1927–28
Thomas, Mark (NC State) DE	1997–98	Vucinich, Milt (Stanford) G	1945
Thomas, Stan (Texas) T	1991–92		
Thompson, Chris (Nichols State) CB	2005	**W**	
Thompson, Russ (Nebraska) T	1936–39	Waddle, Tom (Boston College) WR	1989–94
Thornton, James (California State		Wade, Bobby (Arizona) WR	2003–04
–Fullerton) TE	1988–92	Wade, Charles (Tennessee St.) WR	1974
Thrift, Cliff (E Central Oklahoma) LB	1985	Wade, William (Vanderbilt) QB	1961–66
Thrower, Willie (Michigan State) QB	1953	Waechter, Henry (Nebraska) DE	1982–85
Tillman, Charles (Louisiana Lafayette) DB	2003–05	Wager, Clinton (St. Mary's) E	1942–43
Tillman, Lewis (Jackson State) RB	1994–95	Wagner, Barry (Alabama A&M) WR	1992
Timpson, Michael (Penn State) WR	1995–96	Wagner, Bryan (California State	
Tom, Mel (San Jose State) DE	1973–75	–Northridge) P	1987–88
Tomczak, Mike (Ohio State) QB	1985–90	Wallace, Bob (UTEP) E	1968–72
Torrance, Jack (LSU) T	1939–40	Wallace, John (Notre Dame) E	1928
Trafton, George (Notre Dame) C	1920–32	Wallace, Stan (Illinois) HB	1954–57
Traylor, Keith (Central Oklahoma) DT	2001–03	Walquist, Laurie (Illinois) QB	1922–31
Trimble, Steve (Maryland) DB	1987	Walsh, Steve (Miami, FL) QB	1994–95
Trost, Milt (Marquette) T	1935–39	Walterscheid, Len (S. Utah) S	1977–82
Tucker, Bill (Tennessee State) RB	1971	Ward, John (Oklahoma State) C/G	1976
Tucker, Rex (Texas A&M) G	1999–2002, 2004	Warner, Josh (SUNY–Brockport) T	2003
Tuinei, Van (Arizona) DE	1999–2000	Washington, Fred (TCU) DT	1990
Turner, Cecil (California Poly) FL	1968–73	Washington, Harry (Colorado State) WR	1979
Turner, Clyde (Hardin–Simmons) C	1940–52	Washington, Ted (Louisville) T	2000–02
		Watkins, Bobby (Ohio State) HB	1955–57
U		Watts, Rickey (Tulsa) WR	1979–83
Ulmer, Mike (Doane) CB	1980	Weatherly, Gerald "Bones" (Rice) C	1950, 1952–54
Urlacher, Brian (New Mexico) LB	2000–05	Wells, Mike (Iowa) DT	1998–2000
Usher, Lou (Syracuse) T	1920	Wetnight, Ryan (Stanford) TE	1993–99
		Wetoska, Bob (Notre Dame) T	1960–69
V		Wetzel, Damon (Ohio State) HB	1935
Vactor, Ted (Nebraska) CB	1975	Wheeler, Ted (W. Texas State) G	1970
Vallez, Emilo (New Mexico) TE	1968–69	Wheeler, Wayne (Alabama) WR	1974
Van Horne, Keith (USC) T	1981–93	Whigham, Larry (Northeast Louisiana) S	2000–02
Van Valkenberg, Pete (BYU) RB	1974	Whitaker, Danta (Miss. Valley State) TE	1993
Vasher, Nathan (Texas) CB	2004–05	White, Dez (Georgia Tech) WR	2000–03

White, Lawrence (Dana) WR — 1987

White, Roy (Valparaiso) FB — 1925, 1927–29

White, Wilford (Arizona State) HB — 1951–52

Whitman, S. J. (Tulsa) HB — 1953–54

Whitsell, Dave (Indiana) DB — 1961–66

Whittenton, Jesse (West Texas) HB — 1958

Wiegmann, Casey (Iowa) C/G — 1997–2000

Wightkin, Bill (Notre Dame) DE — 1950–57

Williams, Bob (Notre Dame) QB — 1951–53

Williams, Brock (Notre Dame) CB — 2003

Williams, Brooks (N. Carolina) TE — 1981–82

Williams, Broughton (Florida) T — 1947

Williams, Dave (Colorado) RB — 1979–81

Williams, Fred (Arkansas) T — 1952–63

Williams, James (Cheyney State) T/DT — 1991–2002

Williams, Jeff (Rhode Island) G — 1982

Williams, Oliver (Illinois) WR — 1983

Williams, Perry (Purdue) RB — 1974

Williams, Roosevelt (Tuskegee) CB — 2002

Williams, Tyrone (Wyoming) DT — 1997

Williams, Walt (New Mexico State) CB — 1982–83

Willis, Peter Tom (Florida State) QB — 1990–93

Wilson, George (Northwestern) E — 1937–46

Wilson, Nemiah (Grambling) CB — 1975

Wilson, Otis (Louisville) LB — 1980–87

Wilson, Rod (South Carolina) LB — 2005

Wilson, Troy (Pittsburg State) DE — 2000

Wise, Ty (Miami–FL) C — 2000

Wisne, Jerry (Notre Dame) T — 1999–2000

Wojciechowski, John (Michigan State) T — 1987–93

Wolden, Allan (Bemidji State) RB — 1987

Wooden, Shawn (Notre Dame) S — 2000

Woods, Tony (Oklahoma) DT — 1989

Woolford, Donnell (Clemson) CB — 1989–96

Worley, Tim (Georgia) RB — 1993–94

Worrell, Cameron (Fresno State) S — 2003–05

Wright, Eric (Stephen F. Austin) WR — 1991–92

Wright, Steve (Alabama) T — 1971

Wrightman, Tim (UCLA) TE — 1985–86

Wuerffel, Danny (Florida) QB — 2001

Wynne, Elmer (Notre Dame) FB — 1928

Y

Youmans, Maury (Syracuse) T — 1960–63

Young, Adrian (USC) LB — 1973

Young, Randolph (Millikin) T — 1920

Youngblood, George (LSU) S — 1969

Yourist, Abe (no college) E — 1932

Z

Zanders, Emanuel (Jackson State) G — 1981

Zarnas, Gust (Ohio State) G — 1938

Zawatson, Dave (California) T — 1989

Zeller, Joe (Indiana) G — 1938

Zizak, Vince (Villanova) G — 1934

Zorich, Chris (Notre Dame) DT — 1991–97

Zorich, George (Northwestern) G — 1944–46

Zucco, Vic (Michigan State) HB — 1957–60